# A fresh start
# with God

JOYCE HUGGETT

# A fresh start
# with God

REFLECTIONS FOR LENT

First published in 1991 by Lion Publishing plc

This edition published in 2003 by

KEVIN MAYHEW LTD
Buxhall, Stowmarket, Suffolk, IP14 3BW
E-mail: info@kevinmayhewltd.com

KINGSGATE PUBLISHING INC
1000 Pannell Street, Suite G, Columbia, MO 65201
E-mail: sales@kingsgatepublishing.com

9 8 7 6 5 4 3 2 1 0

ISBN  1 84417 166 3
Catalogue No. 1500656

Cover design by Angela Selfe
Edited by Marian Reid
Typesetting by Louise Selfe

Printed and bound in Great Britain

# Contents

*For Elizabeth*
*with heartfelt thanks*

# Acknowledgements

As I write this, I am in New Zealand, where a friend has just reminded me that we first met each other in 1987 soon after the original edition of this book was published. 'The contents were a great help to me,' this friend observed. I am indebted to her, and to so many other readers, for such support and encouragement.

An author, of course, needs a publisher, and I am so grateful to God for Kevin Mayhew and for the trust he has placed in me. I am grateful, too, for his efficient and friendly team who have reworked the manuscript with me. In particular, I pass on warm thanks to Marian Reid for her affirmation and for her editing skills. It has been a joy to work with her – albeit by phone and e-mail – sometimes across continents.

The prayerful picture meditations have been produced by four of my artist friends: Sr Theresa Margaret CHN, Joan Hutson, Joyce Cheverton and Mandy Patterson. All of the pictures I have selected have been an inspiration to me personally and I am trusting that they will 'speak' to my readers more eloquently than any words of mine.

To each of the above, to those who have given me permission to reproduce photographs of themselves and their baby, and to those who prayed for me while this book was being revised, I give my heartfelt thanks. Finally, warm thanks go to my husband who not only did the cooking while the book was being revised, but who also patiently read and reread the revisions I made, sharpening my thinking with his constructive criticisms.

Each of the above, and the person to whom this book is dedicated, have inspired me to delve deeper into the mystery of the saving love of Jesus. For their faithfulness and trust I shall always be grateful.

Scripture quotations are taken from:

The Good News Bible (GNB), published by the Bible Societies and HarperCollins Publishers, © American Bible Society 1994, used with permission.

Holy Bible, New International Version (NIV), copyright © 1973, 1978, 1984 by International Bible Society. Used by permission of Hodder & Stoughton, a member of the Hodder Headline Group. All rights reserved.

The Jerusalem Bible (JB), published and copyright 1966, 1967 and 1968 by Darton, Longman & Todd Ltd and Doubleday and Co. Inc., and used by permission of the publishers.

Contemporary English Version (CEV), © American Bible Society 1991, 1992, 1995. Used with permission.

The Living Bible (LB), © copyright 1971. Used by permission of Tyndale House Publishers, Inc., Wheaton, IL 60189 USA. All rights reserved.

The New Testament in Modern English, J. B. Phillips (JBP), copyright © HarperCollins Publishers Ltd, Religious Books Division, 77–85 Fulham Palace Road, London W6 8JB. Used by permission.

Illustrations are by:
Joan Hutson (Days 1, 10 and 39); Joyce Cheverton (Day 18); Mandy Patterson (Day 45); Sr Elizabeth Ruth Obard ODC (Day 8); all other illustrations by Sr Theresa Margaret CHN. Photographs are by Ron Tucker (Day 32) and Joyce Huggett.

# Introduction

Some of the material in this book was first published in the 1980s under the title *Approaching Easter* and later under the title *Reflections for Lent*. The book eventually went out of print but, each year since, would-be readers have asked me where they can buy a copy. For this reason, my publisher and I have decided to republish, giving the book a new look and a new title.

*A Fresh Start With God* seemed to be an appropriate title for a Lent book because traditionally, from early on in the history of the Church, Lent – the period that spans Shrove Tuesday (Pancake Day) and Easter Sunday – has always been a time for the kind of recollection that results in remorse, repentance and reconciliation. For this reason, in the Middle Ages, the beginning of Lent was marked by tracing a cross on each believer's forehead. Today, too, in an increasing number of churches and on many retreats, during the Ash Wednesday service, members of the clergy and congregation will have the sign of the cross traced on their foreheads with the ash that has been made from burning last year's palm crosses. Many of us find this a powerful way to begin a prolonged period of reflection as we journey with Jesus into the desert and, eventually, to Calvary and the garden tomb.

Lent is not only a time of repentance. Equally, it is a time of preparation for, and anticipation of, Easter. The place where I have witnessed this happening most effectively is on the island of Cyprus, where my husband and I lived for several years. Our Cypriot neighbours prepared themselves enthusiastically and energetically for the moment when, as Easter Sunday dawned, the whole congregation, packed into the church, would cry out: 'CHRIST IS RISEN!'

One way in which these worshippers prepared for this magnificent cry of joy was by abstaining from meat and dairy products for the whole of Lent. During the second half of Lent, they also spring-cleaned their houses from top to bottom – paintwork was wiped, curtains were washed, carpets and windows cleaned, and so on. Everything had to be in pristine condition to welcome the Risen One.

Sadly, such customs have died out in England. Even so, it seems that an increasing number of Christians find welling up within their hearts a desire to prepare their innermost being for the Risen One. The aim of this book is to suggest some ways in which we may make this fresh start.

Week One of *A Fresh Start With God* focuses on ways of using Lent well. In Week Two we move on, as we place the spotlight first on Jesus' baptism, and then on his sojourn in the Judean desert. In this section, we ask ourselves what can we learn from the lessons he gives us in the desert.

In Week Three we focus on the subject of prayer, since Lent was a time when converts to Christianity learned to pray, asking Jesus to teach *us* to pray. During Week Four the subject under the spotlight is the fruit of the Spirit, as we trust that our observance of Lent will result in us becoming more like Jesus. From the beginning of Week Five we focus on the death of Jesus, asking ourselves what it cost him to die and what his death achieved. The book ends, of course, with the most wonderful news of all time: **Christ is Risen!**

The aim of this book is not to go into any of these vast subjects in too great a depth. Rather, it is to provide readers with a few seminal thoughts which they can turn over in their minds and hearts, feast on, and then respond to. So, each day, there is a verse of Scripture to fuel our meditation, a brief comment for us to contemplate, and at least one prayer to echo. Often, there is also a black and white line drawing or photograph to illustrate the theme of the day.

Since this book is short and, in some ways, undemanding, my

longing is that busy people will use it throughout Lent – on their way to work if they are commuters, over a cup of coffee if they work at home or are housebound, during a lunch or coffee break, or even before work starts if they drive to their office or place of work. I pray that, as they read, a word or an idea, a phrase or a sentence, might worm its way into their hearts so forcefully that, wherever they are, they will want to pray the prayer – or an adaptation of it – and know that they are connecting with the God who is everywhere, the God who suffered, died and rose again to express the enormity of his love for us. If this happens for just one reader, the publishing team and I will rejoice and be assured that the challenge of redesigning this book has not been in vain.

JOYCE HUGGETT

# Making a Fresh Start with God

## Day 1

## Ash Wednesday
## A Time for Spiritual Spring-cleaning

I love the first shafts of sunshine which burst through the windows in spring. Although they show up the layers of dust which have accumulated through the winter and challenge me to start spring-cleaning, they also herald the burgeoning of new life, nature's new start – the wonder of spring.

The original meaning of Lent was 'holy spring'. Traditionally, at this time of year, Christians prepared themselves for Easter by asking God to show them their failures and by repenting of their wrongdoings. People new to Christianity were made ready for their baptism which would take place at Easter. Lent, then, is a time of preparation: a time for spring-cleaning the soul; it is a challenge for us to combat evil in our lives. Lent is also an opportunity to turn back to God. The prophet Joel puts the invitation this way:

'Even now,' declares the Lord,
'return to me with all your heart,
with fasting and weeping and mourning.'

. . . Return to the Lord your God,
for he is gracious and compassionate,
slow to anger and abounding in love . . .
(Joel 2:12, 13, NIV)

Lord God,
forgive me for so often ignoring the grime which soils my life:
the grubby little sins
collecting in the nooks and crannies of my heart;
the cobwebs of guilt hanging from its walls.
Shine your Spirit's light
into the dark, hidden crevices within me.
Expose the murky fantasies, desires, ambitions and hopes
which lurk there.
Help me to deal ruthlessly with anything within
which grieves you.
Strengthen my resolve
to go through with this internal spring-cleaning,
then let me taste afresh your understanding, kind
and patient love.
I praise you for the assurance that,
before I draw near to you, you come close to me;
and that you long for me to enjoy a fresh new start with you.

## Day 2

# A Time for New Beginnings

Lent is a time for new beginnings. New beginnings start with repentance. Repentance is not something negative. True repentance is an active, positive attitude which effects real and deep changes. Repentance involves recognising wrong, and, where possible, putting it right. Repentance is therefore laced with a desire and a determination to live differently. Repentance means honestly facing up to the past and turning from it.

John the Baptist gave this challenge to the crowds who followed him:

Repent, for the kingdom of heaven is near. (Matthew 3:2, NIV)

Jim Wallis, author of *A Call to Conversion*, claims that the biblical meaning of repentance is far richer than the word that is in common usage today. The word *we* use suggests that we should be sorry or feel guilty about something we have done or thought or said. In the New Testament, however, 'to repent' means to turn our backs on sin and selfishness, on darkness and idols, on bad habits and bondages – both private and public – and to make a brand-new start in life.

In other words, repentance involves us in making a U-turn *away* from anything which involves violence or evil. In fact, repentance means turning away from the powers of death. Repentance and receiving God's forgiveness go hand in hand. As John puts it in his first epistle:

If we confess our sins, he is faithful and just and will forgive our sins and purify us from all unrighteousness.
(1 John 1:9, NIV)

When we confess, then, we must also move on to receive and embrace God's forgiveness and love. To fail to do so implies that we give greater importance to our sinful self than we do to God's

goodness. We must learn to accept that God's goodness is greater than our badness; that there is joy in God's heart in extending to us the forgiving love which sets us free from our past sin. We must refuse to nurse a sense of guilt and accept the healing God offers.

*I come to you, dear God,*
*sin-stained and weary, hopelessly handicapped*
*by my own failures.*
*Yet I know you do not want me to nurse a sense of guilt*
*or inferiority;*
*you want me to shed my burden*
*so that I can be released and cleansed from it.*
*Here and now, I lay that burden on you, the burden-bearer.*

*There I leave it as I go*
*to make amends for the*
*hurt I have caused*
*. . . and . . .*
*May I love them*
*with your pure,*
*reconciling love.*

*Lord,*
*you come to me,*
*you touch me,*
*you wipe away my*
*tears,*
*you smile at me.*
*Embrace me;*
*you iron out my fears.*
*Thank you.*

## Day 3

# A Time to Come Back

Lent can be a glorious forty-day retreat. A retreat is a time to stand back, to ask ourselves:

- What have I been doing with my life?
- What has God been teaching me?
- Where have I succeeded in living life God's way?
- Where have I failed?
- What do I need to confess to God, or to change?

A Lenten retreat is a time to recognise our wanderings and to determine to heed God's call to come back:

'But now, now – it is the Lord who speaks – come back to me with all your heart . . . turn to the Lord your God again, for he is all tenderness and compassion, slow to anger, rich in graciousness.          (Joel 2:12, 13, JB – slightly adapted)

Like the young man in the story of the prodigal son, Jesus, I make a calculated choice to come back to you and your Father. I echo the prodigal's prayer: I will get up and go to my father and say, 'Father, I have sinned against God and against you. I am no longer fit to be called your son' (Luke 15:18, GNB).

Like the young man in this story, Lord, I marvel at your response:

When he was still a long way off, his father saw him. His heart pounding, he ran out, embraced him, and kissed him . . . 'Quick! Bring a clean set of clothes and dress him. Put the family ring on his finger and sandals on his feet. Then get a grain-fed heifer and roast it. We're going to feast! We're going to have a wonderful time!'      (Luke 15:20, 22, The Message)

For your tenderness to *me*,
for your compassion for *me*,
for being so gracious to *me*, dear Lord,
I give you humble and heartfelt thanks.

You are my peace, dear Lord.
In the countless pressures of daily life,
in its disappointments and rejections,
its hectic and senseless haste,
I come to you and find acceptance and shalom.
The clamour dies;
I come to life in the sunshine of your presence.
Come afresh to this soul of mine.

## Day 4

# A Time to Hope

Unending love is what God is. Lent is a time to experience that love. For this reason, God 'woos' us and assures us that though we have failed him, he will not forsake us. He has expressed this powerfully through the prophet Hosea:

> My people are hell-bent on leaving me . . .
> How can I give up on you? . . .
> How can I leave you to be ruined? . . .
> I can't bear to even think such thoughts.
> My insides churn in protest . . .
> And why?
> Because I am God and not a human.
> I am the Holy One and I am here – in your very midst.
> (Hosea 11:7-10, The Message)

Such passionate commitment requires a response. Lent is a good time to make that response to God in the way he requests:

> Return to the Lord your God and let this prayer be your offering to him: 'Forgive all our sins and accept our prayer, and we will praise you as we have promised.'                    (Hosea 14:2)

God's love is perfect, and so when we return to him in the way he asks, we enjoy unending security. He has promised that he will never abandon us nor banish us from his presence.

> Can a mother forget the baby at her breast and have no compassion on the child she has borne? Though she may forget, I will not forget you! See, I have engraved you on the palms of my hands.                    (Isaiah 49:15, 16, NIV)

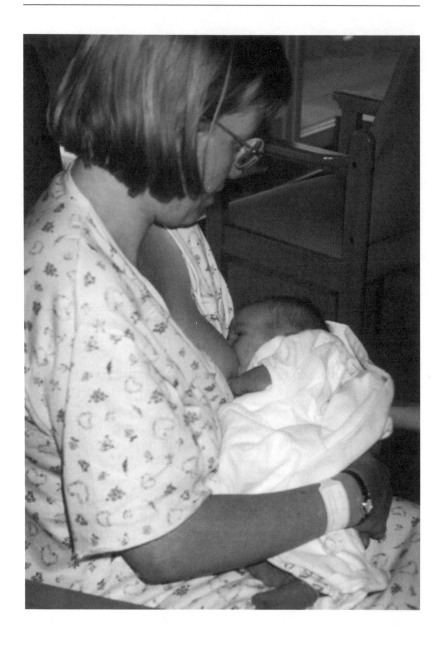

When such promises cause hope and confidence to spring up afresh in our hearts we can echo this prayer with integrity:

*Loving Lord,*
*your love compels me, draws me close.*
*Hear the prayer of my heart,*
*receive my cry of repentance.*

*Be merciful to me, O God,*
*because of your constant love.*
*Because of your great mercy,*
*wipe away my sins!*
*Wash away all that stains my soul.*
*Remove my sin, and I shall be clean;*
*wash me, and I shall be whiter than snow.*

*Let me hear again the sounds of joy and gladness;*
*and though you have crushed and broken me,*
*I will be happy once again.*
*Create a pure heart in me, O God,*
*and put a new and loyal spirit in me . . .*
*give me again the joy that comes from your salvation*
*and make me willing to obey you.*

*Help me to speak, Lord,*
*and I will praise you.*
*You will not reject a humble and repentant heart.*
*Thank you.*

Child,
place the fabric of your life
in the vat of my love.
Watch as I withdraw the stains of sin;
know that my grace makes you pure within.
Rejoice, for in me you will never be rejected –
but always accepted, and uniquely loved.

Week Two

# Jesus: Tempted Just Like Us

## Day 5

## The Baptism of Jesus

Lent is a time to refocus – to turn away from the busyness which preoccupies us for most of the year and to concentrate on Jesus. Today we focus on his baptism. As Matthew describes it:

> Then Jesus came from Galilee to the Jordan to be baptised by John.                                  (Matthew 3:13, NIV)

For thirty years, Jesus had lived the life of an obscure carpenter in Nazareth. He knew, though, that his mission in life extended beyond this little town tucked away in the hills. He knew that he had come to rescue men and women from the tyranny of their own sin. Jesus chose to leave Nazareth and to make his first public appearance in the wake of the wave of repentance which swept through Galilee as a result of the teaching of John the Baptist.

Like hundreds of others, Jesus was baptised by John. Unlike the others, though, he was not baptised as a sign that he repented of his sin. Jesus was sinless. He had no need to repent. Nevertheless, he identified with sinful mankind by descending into the green waters of the River Jordan. As he emerged from this beautiful river, he was deep in prayer. The heavens opened. The Holy Spirit fluttered down on him in the form of a dove. And he heard the Father's voice commissioning him: 'You are my Son, chosen and marked by my love, pride of my life' (Luke 3:22, The Message). In other words, 'You are the Messiah.'

Jesus knew that he was receiving the fullness of the Spirit to equip him for the task God had given him to do: to save the world from the clutches of the Evil One. He walked away from the river determined to build God's kingdom on earth. He recognised that he was the kingdom's designated, qualified and ordained King.

To be the Messiah would involve suffering and death: death on a cross. Jesus knew that. Instead of flinching in the face of such pain, he accepted it out of love for his Father and for mankind. He knew that the only way to rescue mankind was to die in their place on the tree of Calvary.

Lord Jesus,
when pain rises over the horizon
and threatens to engulf me,
I recoil in terror.
So I stand awestruck as I watch you choose
not life, but death;
not glory, but grief;
not joy, but sorrow;
not a crown, but a cross.

I marvel even more as I recall that:
you were pierced for my faults,
crushed for my sins:
on you was being laid
a punishment that brings me peace.
Because of your wounds
I enjoy healing.
Such knowledge is too vast for me to grasp.
As I drink it in
I worship you in wonder, love and praise.

## Day 6

# The Testing of Jesus

It has been said that temptation is a test which often comes to a person whom God is preparing to use. The word 'temptation' really means 'testing'. Just as metal must be tested far beyond any strain or stress that will ever be placed on it before it can be considered reliable, so we have to be tested before God can use us in any major way. During the first part of Lent, we focus on the way Jesus was tested in the wilderness. Matthew sums it up succinctly when he writes:

> Then Jesus was led by the Spirit into the desert to be tempted by the devil. (Matthew 4:1, NIV)

The word Matthew uses for 'led' can also be translated 'thrust': 'Jesus was *thrust* by the Spirit into the desert.' Here, instead of being surrounded by crowds on the banks of the River Jordan, he finds himself in the howling desert where he is completely alone except for the wild beasts. The Spirit has steered him from the devout acclaim of his cousin John the Baptist to the utter forsakenness of the desert. The audible approval of the heavenly Father is replaced by the vicious assaults of the devil.

This fierce contest between good and evil took place in a vast arena where the hills are bare and desolate and where the limestone blisters under the fierce sun. The rocks stand stark and jagged, and there are precipices well over a thousand feet high which drop down to the Dead Sea. In this awesome but terrifying place, Jesus was sorely tempted.

Michel Quoist explains why the person who desires to live for God will also be tested. One reason is that such longings are despicable to the Evil One who is far from pleased when a Christian chooses to live for God and for others rather than for self. For this reason, he ensures that, from time to time, such people feel the terror and the tug of temptation. God, in his wisdom, allows this to happen – not so that his loved one should be defeated, but so that she or he might learn to depend on and trust him more fully.

At such times, as experience quickly reveals, we dare not 'go it alone'. We need God to keep us from falling. The Psalmist puts this persuasively and powerfully when he asks:

Who can discern his lapses and errors?
Clear me from hidden [and unconscious] faults . . .

Let the words of my mouth and the meditation of my heart
be acceptable in your sight,
O Lord, my [firm, impenetrable] rock and my redeemer.

(Psalm 19:12-14*)

---

* The Amplified Bible, Zondervan Bible Publishers, 1965

## Day 7

# The Self-denial of Jesus

In today's world we are familiar with the hunger strike through which a person or organisation seeks to gain political power. We are accustomed, too, to people starving themselves to death to attract attention to a cause they believe in. Jesus, Matthew tells us, 'fasted for forty days and forty nights'. Matthew states the obvious when he reminds us that this forty-day fast:

> . . . left him, of course, in a state of extreme hunger, which the devil took advantage of in the first test.
>
> (Matthew 4:2, The Message)

Many men and women before Jesus had fasted: Moses, the lawgiver; King David; Queen Esther; to name a few. People of God denied themselves food for several reasons:

- to express their love for God;
- to focus fully on God;
- to seek to discover God's will for their lives.

This is what Jesus is doing in the wilderness: giving himself to prayer, listening intently to his Father's instructions, seeking to discover how God wants him to rescue mankind from the clutches of the Evil One.

While Jesus was focusing on God in this way, Satan sidled up to him and did his utmost to dissuade Jesus from doing God's work in God's way. While he fasts, Jesus engages in 'spiritual warfare'.

The Christian, too, is caught up in a cosmic struggle against evil. Paul gives a clear warning of this salutary fact:

> We are not fighting against human beings but against the wicked spiritual forces in the heavenly world, the rulers, authorities, and cosmic powers of this dark age. (Ephesians 6:12, GNB)

The spiritual retreat of Lent challenges us to benefit from fasting also. By giving up a meal once a week, or all food for one day each week, or by depriving ourselves of a luxury – such as a television programme we enjoy – we, too, can give ourselves to leisurely prayer and listening to God. God may use this time to highlight inconsistencies in our life, to challenge us to change and to show us more of himself. He will also reveal to us the depth of his love for us.

*Grant me, O Lord,*
*to know what is worth knowing,*
*to love what is worth loving,*
*to praise what delights you most,*
*to value what is precious*
*in your sight,*
*to hate what is offensive to you.*
*Do not let me judge*
*by what I see,*
*nor pass sentence according to*
*what I hear,*
*but rather to judge rightly between*
*things that differ,*
*and above all to search out*
*and to do what pleases you,*
*through Jesus Christ our Lord.*

*Thomas a Kempis (1380–1471)*

# Day 8

# Subtle Persuasions

The wilderness where Satan and Jesus were engaged in spiritual warfare was littered with little bits of limestone which look rather like pitta bread: round and flat and creamy-white in colour. Since Jesus had not eaten for nearly six weeks, he was very hungry. Satan used that very moment to sidle alongside the Son of God to try to trip him up. As Matthew puts it:

> The tempter came and said to him, 'If you are the Son of God, tell these stones to turn into loaves.' (Matthew 4:3, JB)

The temptation was subtle. Bread is the staple diet of many people in the world. If Jesus had been detected turning stones into bread, people would have flocked to him – not because he was the Messiah, but because he met their material needs. Despite his own need for food, Jesus recognised the ploy for what it was – a temptation to woo people with bribery, to win them with popularity, and to use his God-given gifts to meet his own earthly needs. Jesus knew, though, that he had not come to earth for any of these. So he rebuked the enemy who was scheming to persuade him to depart from his mission.

Satan not only tempted Jesus to bribe the people to worship him and to use his miraculous powers to meet his own needs, he went on to challenge Jesus' divinity, mocking the Messiah with this sneer: 'If you are the Son of God . . .'

'If you are the Son of God'? Jesus knew without a shadow of doubt that he was, indeed, God's Son. Had not his Father reminded him of this fact at his baptism? Instead of allowing himself to be tripped up by the wiles of the Evil One, he used his reactions to the temptations to clarify the methods he *would* use to woo people for God. The temptations, then, far from heralding his downfall, helped him to clarify in his own mind which methods he would choose and which he would reject when he returned to the mission he had come to fulfil.

17

Having rejected once and for all the pathway to popularity, bribery and personal pleasure, he reaffirmed his determination to do God's work in God's way – to obey *God's* promptings, even though these involved accepting the way of suffering and, ultimately, death on the Cross.

Satan's methods have not changed. He uses the same ploys to trip up Christians today. He tries to persuade us that God cannot possibly love us. He tries to persuade us to use our talents, possessions and personalities for pure pleasure and self-gratification instead of dedicating them to God. So the challenge of Lent that St Teresa summed up so well comes to every Christian: 'How long will it be before we imitate this great God in any way?'

*Jesus,*
*your example fills me with awe.*
*You won this round against Satan,*
*you set me an example:*
*to stand up to the devil*
*when he whispers in my ear.*
*You triumphed over evil;*
*with your help, I can do the same.*
*By your grace, I will.*


O Jesus, I have promised
to serve thee to the end;
be thou for ever near me,
my Master and my Friend;
I shall not fear the battle
if thou art by my side,
nor wander from the pathway
if thou wilt be my guide.

O let me feel thee near me;
the world is ever near;
I see the sights that dazzle,
the tempting sounds I hear;
my foes are ever near me,
around me and within;
but, Jesus, draw thou nearer,
and shield my soul from sin.

*John Ernest Bode (1816–1874)*

## Day 9

# Subtle Temptations

The Spirit of God had thrust Jesus into the wilderness. Satan now carries him to Jerusalem. Matthew describes it in this way:

> The devil then took (Jesus) to the holy city and made him stand on the parapet of the Temple. 'If you are the Son of God,' he said, 'throw yourself down . . .' Jesus said to him, '. . . You must not put the Lord your God to the test.'     (Matthew 4:5-7, JB)

Jesus was standing on the highest part of the Temple. In all probability, he was perched at the corner of this magnificent building looking down on the valley below – a sheer drop of four hundred and fifty feet. The time was probably daybreak so blasts from the priests' silver trumpets would be heralding a new day and Jerusalem would be thronging with people.

'Jump,' taunts Satan. 'Let everyone see your Father catch you in his arms. Hasn't he promised to send his angels to watch over you in times of danger?'

If Jesus had leapt, like superman, from this pinnacle, his fame would have spread through Jerusalem like wildfire. He would have won the applause, adulation and admiration of everyone. However, Jesus firmly resisted the temptation to become a sensationalist by drawing attention to himself through the miracles he performed. He silenced the enemy with the reminder from Scripture: 'Do not put the Lord your God to the test' (Matthew 4:7, JB).

As William Barclay once reminded us, by refusing to succumb to this temptation, Jesus determined to demonstrate that it is irresponsible to see how far you can go with God. It is equally irresponsible to deliberately, recklessly and needlessly place your-self in a threatening situation and then to expect God to rescue you from it. God *is* capable of performing such a miracle, of course, but his rescuing power must never be viewed as a toy to play with or something to experiment with. Rather, it is an aspect of God's nature to be trusted.

*Jesus,*
*you experienced the full force of temptation,*
*yet you conquered it in the fight against Satan.*
*Breathe into my life the strength of your Holy Spirit*
*that I may also expose evil constantly,*
*confront Satan valiantly,*
*and come out of such conflict victoriously.*
*In every moment of testing, may I stand fast as you did.*
*In the challenge to combat evil in my life,*
*may I grow neither faint nor weary*
*but rather persevere to the end;*
*until I hear your 'Well done, good and faithful servant'.*

## Day 10

# Subtle Suggestions

Satan does not give up easily. He tried to persuade Jesus to bribe people into the kingdom of God by simply meeting their material needs. He also tried to encourage Jesus to attract attention to himself through the spectacular, to use magic to bring people to God. Having failed in both these attempts, he then challenged Jesus' integrity with a third suggestion. Luke describes it in this way:

> Finally, the devil took Jesus up on a very high mountain and showed him all the kingdoms on earth and their power. The devil said to him, 'I will give all this to you, if you will bow down and worship me.'
> Jesus answered, 'Go away Satan! The Scriptures say: "Worship the Lord your God and serve only him."' (Matthew 4:8, CEV)

Jesus had eaten nothing for six weeks. He was physically weak. He knew that he faced the gargantuan task of winning the world for his Father; of snatching it back from the clutches of the Evil One. Satan chose this moment of vulnerability to take Jesus out into God's wonderful world. There on a mountain top they viewed the splendour of God's creation in all its glory. How could one man capture all this for God?

22

Into Jesus' mind Satan whispers an idea: 'Worship me and I will give all of this to you. Your task will be easy.'

What the tempter is whispering here may be summed up in one word: compromise. By stooping to the moral standards accepted by the world as the norm, Jesus could have attracted a great following! 'Why don't you strike a bargain with me?' suggests Satan. 'Change the world by becoming like the people who live in it. Then they will follow you in great numbers.'

Jesus' refusal was curt: 'Beat it, Satan!' He backed his rebuke with a third quotation from Deuteronomy: 'Worship the Lord your God, and only him. Serve him with absolute single-heartedness.'
(Matthew 4:10, The Message)

Jesus knew that he could never defeat evil by compromising with evil. He was called to be a light that beams its rays into the world's darkness, not to become part of that darkness. His task was to raise men's standards until they were brought into perfect alignment with God's. Nothing less than this would satisfy him or his Father. Once again, the result of this temptation is that Jesus submits himself to the Father. He determines to do God's work in God's way.

---

Be off, Satan,
from this door and from these four walls.
This is no place for you;
there is nothing for you to do here.
This is the place for Jesus and the gospel;
and this is where I mean to sleep.*

* An adaptation of one of the earliest Christian prayers recorded.
Veronica Zundell (compiler), *The Lion Book of Famous Prayers*
(Oxford, Lion Publishing, 1983).

## Day 11

# Tempted! Just Like Me!

Revd Michael Green once suggested that, during Jesus' forty-day retreat in the desert, Satan aimed to drive a wedge between Jesus and his Father. In order to achieve this aim, he used several tactics: doubt, disobedience, distrust, disloyalty, compromise, exhibitionism, idolatry and tempting Jesus to short-circuit Calvary.

Today, Satan's target is Christians. They stand in Satan's line of fire. The author of the letter to the Hebrews spells out some very good news:

> Because [Jesus] himself suffered when he was tempted, he is able to help those who are being tempted.     (Hebrews 2:18, NIV)

Satan is always on the rampage. The more we try to please God, the more he will seek to sidetrack us. As Peter puts it:

> Be on your guard and stay awake. Your enemy, the devil, is like a roaring lion, prowling around to find someone to attack.
> (1 Peter 5:8, CEV)

Satan selects a variety of ways to bring about our downfall. He tests us through our feelings, for one thing. On the days when we cannot feel God's presence, he tries to persuade us that God has abandoned us; that he is a God who is more absent than present. He would even tempt us to doubt God's trustworthiness. These lies are to be rejected.

The tempter is also capable of using our innermost thoughts and desires to bring about our downfall. He launches his attack against our mind, our will and our passions so that even though we know that a certain course of action is not permissible for the Christian, we do it; even though we know that a certain place is riddled with temptation, we go there. In this way, Satan so often wins another round in the eternal conflict between good and evil in our lives.

At other times, our enemy confuses us so much that we don't know whether we want to obey God or not. Michel Quoist expressed this confusion powerfully on one occasion. In a prayer he confessed that he was at the end of his tether, shattered, broken. He admitted that he was struggling with a temptation that sometimes seemed subtle, sometimes persuasive, sometimes tender and sometimes sensuous. He also admitted that he neither knew what to do nor where to go. Even if he tried to escape it by leaving one room, he found it waiting for him in the next.

His honest prayer finds an echo in the hearts of countless Christians worldwide.

The season of Lent challenges us to rediscover ways of combating and triumphing over the enemy as Jesus did. Jesus defeated Satan by confounding his lies with the truth found in the Bible. For this reason, Martin Luther also used to advise his followers to quote Scripture when they were tempted. If that failed, he advised them to jeer and flout Satan because he cannot bear scorn.

*It seems almost a law of life, dear Lord,*
*that, after every great moment I experience,*
*I swing from the stars to the mud.*

*While I am struggling in the mud of my own defeat*
*Satan seems to sidle up to me, accusing me,*
*using my weariness and discouragement,*
*my moods and my depressions,*
*to cause me to doubt you.*
*Teach me to resist the devil, Lord, just as you did.*
*Cause me to be vigilant,*
*conscious that he is ever ready to trip me up.*
*Give me the grace to triumph over him as you did,*
*by submitting to the Father's will.*

Week Three

# Jesus, the Man of Prayer

## Day 12

## The Transfiguration

The Bible readings traditionally used by Christians during Lent move swiftly from focusing on the humanity of Jesus to the contemplation of his 'otherness', his divinity:

> . . . Jesus took Peter, John and James with him and went up on a mountain to pray. While he was praying, his face changed, and his clothes became shining-white. Suddenly Moses and Elijah were there speaking with him. They appeared in heavenly glory and talked about all that Jesus' death in Jerusalem would mean.
>
> Peter and the other two disciples had been sound asleep. All at once they woke up and saw how glorious Jesus was. They also saw the two men who were with him.
>
> Moses and Elijah were about to leave, when Peter said to Jesus: 'Master, it is good for us to be here! Let us make three shelters, one for you, one for Moses and one for Elijah' . . .
>
> While Peter was still speaking, a shadow from a cloud passed over them, and they were frightened as the cloud covered them. From the cloud a voice spoke, 'This is my chosen Son. Listen to what he says!' (Luke 9:28-35, CEV).

I once visited the Mount of Transfiguration with a group of pilgrims. All of us were awestruck as we meditated together on this miraculous moment in Jesus' life. Many of us could imagine the cloud descending, indicating how near God was. Many of us could well imagine the sound of the Father's voice proclaiming how much he loved and valued his Son. Each of us contemplated, in our own way, the transfigured form of Jesus: his body enveloped with the light of God, his face radiating the glory of God and his clothing shining with a whiteness the human eye could scarcely tolerate.

Lent provides us with the challenge and opportunity to drink in these mysteries:

- the mystery of who God is;
- the mystery of God's greatness;
- the mystery of his humility in taking on himself a human form.

You are holy, Lord, the only God,
and your deeds are wonderful.
You are strong, you are great.
You are the most High, you are almighty.
You, holy Father, are King of heaven and earth.
You are Three and One, Lord God, all good.
You are good, all good, supreme good.
You are love, you are wisdom.
You are humility, you are endurance.
You are rest, you are peace.
You are joy and gladness, you are justice and moderation.
You are all our riches, and you suffice us.
You are beauty, you are gentleness.
You are our protector, you are our guardian and defender.
You are courage, you are our haven and our hope.
You are our faith, our great consolation.
You are our eternal life, great and wonderful Lord,
God almighty, merciful Saviour.

*Francis of Assisi (1181–1226)*

## Day 13

# Lord, Teach Us to Pray

Jesus' disciples could see for themselves that the quality of Jesus' prayer was different from any form of prayer they had encountered before. One day they begged him: 'Lord, teach us to pray' (Luke 11:1, NIV). Lent, the special season set apart for reflection and prayer, the weeks for making a fresh start with God, is a good time to reiterate that request and to act on Jesus' basic advice:

> When you pray, go into a room alone and close the door. Pray to your Father in private.                    (Matthew 6:6, CEV)

People who are serious about learning to pray hold two things in tension: the fact that it is possible to pray at any time and in any place and the fact that there is great value in heeding Jesus' advice and earmarking a certain place for regular prayer: it might be a corner of the bedroom, a certain chair in the lounge, a quiet room in the house, a church or a particular walk or spot in the garden. We know that when we retreat to that place it is for one purpose only: the serious, privileged business of prayer.

Prayer, essentially, is developing a relationship with God. Friends find time and places to meet. If we are serious about forging a friendship with God, we will do what he says: prepare a meeting place where the friendship can deepen and grow. The more we meet God in the silence of this specific place of prayer, the more we shall learn to recognise his presence elsewhere: in nature, while walking, driving, ironing, gardening or talking to friends and neighbours.

*Dear Lord, teach me to pray –*
*for just as the deer pants for cool water,*
*so my heart hungers for you.*
*My soul is parched and dry,*
*I thirst for a sense of your presence:*
*I will carve out a place for you.*
*Lord, hear my prayer,*
*in that place –*
*in every place –*
*come to me and meet me.*

Day 14

# To Pray Like Jesus

In answer to the disciples' request: 'Lord, teach us to pray', Jesus said: 'Say this when you pray: Father . . .' (Luke 11:2, NIV). No one had ever prayed like Jesus because no one in the whole world had ever been conscious, as he was, that God was his Father – that God's love for him was total. When Jesus prayed, he frequently called God 'Abba' – 'Daddy'. He implores those of us who are his disciples to do the same: to turn our eyes to God with childlike trust and to simply whisper that intimate little word: 'Daddy'.

A good father cherishes his child. A good father gives his child security, stability, guidance and unconditional love. A good father makes sacrifices for his child. A good father delights in every stage of his child's growth.

The desert-dweller, Carlo Carretto, expressed this beautifully when he testified to his own deep-down awareness that the God of the universe whom he worshipped with awe was also the father who cherished him, looked after him and loved him. Such was the extent of this fatherly love that God gave his child precious gifts: life, truth and love. Since he could trust implicitly in this love, Carlo Carretto could remain calm and live in peace. In his innermost being he knew that he was secure for life and for death, for time and for eternity. In God, his father, he found his true dignity and worth. No matter what the future held for him or what happened to him, nothing could erase the fact that God was his father.

Since God was his father, prayer became, for Carlo Carretto, the place where consciously he would call God 'Father'. Indeed, prayer was the place where he experienced intimacy with God and where he knew himself loved and held and met by his heavenly Father. When praying, he became conscious that God came to him, wiped away his tears, healed his hurts and enfolded him in his arms of love.

Father,
in this place of prayer
I feel your everlasting arms
enfolding me,
caressing me,

in the embrace of never-ending love.
For this tenderness
I praise you.
That I am the focus of your love
I thank you.
That you have deigned to call me your child
I adore you,
and surrender myself to you,
though all too feeble
is my response of love to Love.

Day 15

# A Unique Relationship

A vital ingredient of any developing friendship is time. If our relationship with God is to develop, grow and mature, it is essential that we give God quality time. During Lent, many Christians make sacrifices to increase the amount of time available for giving undivided attention to God. Jesus tells us what to do with this time:

'You should pray like this:
Our Father in heaven,
may your holy name be honoured . . . '
(Matthew 6:9, GNB)

The word 'holy' means 'different', 'unique', 'other', and the phrase 'God's name' means much more than a brand or a label. 'God's name' sums up his entire personality. In other words, Jesus seems to be suggesting that in our thinking as well as in our relating, God should be treated differently from everyone else we know. God should be given a position in our lives that is absolutely unique. God is to be reverenced.

If we truly pray this part of the Lord's Prayer, it will mean that we endeavour to live our lives in constant awareness of God. On those days when we succeed in this, the world will seem so God-filled that our hearts will respond with awe and gratitude as we find ourselves in touch with his greatness, his tenderness, his compassion, his beauty and his love. Nature will provide these reminders; so will the face and trust of a child; and so might the joy of someone caught up in the worship of God.

Lent is the season to concentrate on increasing our ability to be conscious of God's presence inside us and beside us. As a friend of mine used to remind us, as we work, we may become aware of a Loved Presence peering over our shoulder or, as we drive, we could be conscious of the same Loved Presence travelling beside us. This same loving Companion is with us, too, when we are reading or cooking, studying or teaching, nursing or doing the accounts. He is also there in the maelstrom of the supermarket or in the queue for a bus or train. The more we become conscious of this all-encompassing, all-loving Presence, the more our days will be filled with a healthy nostalgia for our ever-loving Creator.

Father –
Holy,
Revered,
Mysterious is your Name.
May all my contacts and relationships,
my struggles and temptations,
my thoughts, dreams and desires,
be coloured by the loving reverence I have for you.
May your personality be reflected
in my work,
in the words of my lips,
and in the thoughts that lodge in my mind –
so that all I am,
and all I do,
may become ever more worthy
of your holy presence
living in me.

God be in my head and in my understanding,
God be in my eyes and in my looking,
God be in my mouth and in my speaking,
God be in my tongue and in my tasting,
God be in my lips and in my greeting . . .
God be in my ears and in my hearing,
God be in my neck and in my humbling . . .
God be in my hands and in my working . . .
God be in my end and at my reviving.

Pynson's *Horae*, 1514

## Day 16

# Your Will Be Done

When Jesus was coaching his disciples in the art and the ABC of praying, he said:

'This is how you should pray: ". . . your will be done".'
(Matthew 6:9, 10, NIV)

At the nub of true prayer lies obedience. In fact, we can scarcely think about prayer without thinking about obedience. Obedience means the relinquishment of *my will* – my longings, my desires, my choices – and the acceptance of God's will: his longings, his desires, his choices. Obedience involves my will being brought into complete alignment with the will of God.

Jesus could teach others this prayer of obedience because he was obedient to his Father in every detail of his life. Indeed, Jesus delighted to submit his will to the Father's will. He well knew that his Father's will, far from being something menacing, had his best intentions at heart. Instead of seeking to escape from this will, then, Jesus accepted it even when it hurt him to do so. This kind of obedience demonstrates the faith he had in the fact that God's plans are always loving and right.

The father of a newborn baby once expressed to me his feelings for his wife and child: 'I've never loved anyone like this before. I can think of no one but them. I just want to be with them doing whatever I can for them. When they are distressed, I am distressed. When they are happy, I am happy. Nothing else matters to me – only them.'

God's love for us is like that. God's longing and desire, love and joy are focused on his people. He delights in them. He safeguards them. He yearns over them. That is why the Christian can say with confidence, in the words of Julian of Norwich: 'I saw that [God] is to us everything that is good.'

Lord,
you know what I desire,
but I desire it only if it is your will that I should have it.
If it is not your will, good Lord,
do not be displeased,
for my will is to do your will.

*Julian of Norwich (c. 1342-1413)*

Day 17

# Forgive Us . . . As We Forgive

When the disciples asked Jesus to teach them to pray, he gave them clear instructions:

'You should pray like this . . . "Forgive us the wrongs we have done as we forgive the wrongs that others have done to us."'
(Matthew 6:12, GNB)

And he adds a warning to these strict instructions:

'If you forgive others the wrongs they have done to you, your Father in heaven will also forgive you. But if you do not forgive others, then your Father will not forgive the wrongs you have done.'
(Matthew 6:14, GNB)

Jesus expects us to obey these exhortations all the year round. Many of us live life at such a pace, though, that it is all too easy to fail to recognise where lack of forgiveness has taken up residence in our hearts. Lent is an excellent opportunity to make a fresh start by inviting God to put his finger on any relationship which has turned sour or on any bitterness or resentment against people which may have been poisoning our lives. When he places his spotlight on such emotions, we need to ask him for the grace to tip out the rubble that has collected in our lives so that God can fill us anew with his life.

If we are to be fully motivated to do this, it is important that we understand what forgiveness is and what it is not.

Forgiveness is not a matter of fuzzy, warm emotions. It is a function of the will. It is not asking the question *'Can* I forgive?' but rather, 'With God's help, *will* I forgive?'

Forgiveness refuses to pretend that a particular person has not injured or upset us in some way. True forgiveness is usually granted in two stages. The first stage involves recalling the full extent of the hurt that has been inflicted and even admitting at least to ourselves: 'Yes, that hurt.' In the second stage we move on from here to determine that, although it hurt, 'We *will* forgive . . . '

To forgive means to drop, to let go of, any resentment, bitterness, hatred, or unnecessary anger that we have been harbouring. To forgive means letting a person off the hook – cancelling the debt we feel we are owed. With God's help, we *can* forgive, albeit, often only with a struggle.

Anthony Bloom reminds us why we put up such a struggle. One reason is that, when we say we forgive someone, what we actually mean is that we are putting that person on probation. Impatiently, we wait for that person to show remorse or repentance. We also wait for them to change. We try to ensure that the person has mended his or her ways. This is often a lose-lose situation because it can take a lifetime to fully effect the necessary changes. What Jesus commands us to do is to drop our resentments unreservedly. He also reminds us that, until we have forgiven the person(s) who has harmed us, we ourselves are not forgiven. These are hard words indeed but, by God's grace, it *is* possible – even liberating – to live life the Jesus way.

My child,
I see the pockets of poison that have collected inside you.

Here and now I lance the abscess,
drain it of its pus,
and cleanse you through and through.
Receive my love afresh.
Let it wash right through you,
cleansing you.
Carry it to those you secretly despised.
My love alone bears
the healing grace of reconciliation.

*O Lord, my God, I cried to you for help, and you have healed me (Psalm 30:2). Thank you, Father.*

*Lord, I want to make a fresh start with you this Lent.*
*In that way it can be a true preparation for Easter:*
*a letting out of all that cannot coexist*
*with your love in my life.*
*As I reread your challenge –*
*'Forgive! Forgive! Forgive!' –*
*I am aware that I have been withholding forgiveness*
*from (name) and (name) and (name) because of . . .*
*Because you require it of me, my dear Lord,*
*I forgive them now.*
*I let them off the hook.*
*Forgive me for having borne these grudges for so long.*
*See in my heart the poison of bitterness,*
*resentment and hatred that I have stored there,*
*fingering it from time to time*
*with ghoulish pleasure.*
*Here and now, before you, the living God,*
*I repent of my negativity*
*and beg your forgiveness.*
*Wash me and I shall be whiter than snow.*

## Day 18

# Praying Now

Jesus' life and ministry of prayer did not stop when he ascended to heaven. The writer to the Hebrews assures us that Jesus' prayer-life is ever active and ever effective:

> He is able, now and always, to save those who come to God through him, because he lives for ever to plead with God for them. (Hebrews 7:25, GNB)

> Christ . . . went into heaven itself, where he now appears on our behalf in the presence of God. (Hebrews 9:24, GNB)

Jesus' prayer-life on earth was unique. His prayer-life today is more amazing still. I like to remind myself of this by displaying in my study these reassuring words: 'Jesus is praying for me now.' The thought that Jesus is stationed in heaven at the Father's throne praying for us continuously is an awesome one. We are assured, however, that this is Jesus' ongoing ministry. Since Jesus is *the* man of prayer, we can, as it were, draw alongside him when we pray and stand with him in the Father's presence. In this way we break through the limitations of time and space with the certainty that our prayers *will* be both heard and honoured.

Christians down the ages have considered Lent to be an ideal time to ensure that they carve out time for this priceless privilege of praying alongside the man of prayer, Jesus himself.

Lord God, living and true:
you are love,
you are wisdom,
you are humility,
you are endurance,
you are rest,
you are peace,
you are joy and gladness,
you are justice and moderation,
you are all our riches,
and you suffice for us.
You are beauty,
you are gentleness,
you are our protector,
you are our guardian and defender,
you are courage,
you are our haven and our hope,
you are our faith,
our great consolation.
You are our eternal life,
great and wonderful Lord,
God almighty,
Merciful Saviour.

*St Francis of Assisi (1181–1776)*

For the privilege of praying to you,
I give you thanks.

Week Four

# The Fruit of the Spirit

## Day 19

## The Harvest of the Spirit

One cold, grey November day I was asked to meet a friend from
the station in the town where I then lived. When I arrived, to my
surprise, the normally cheerless foyer of the station had been
completely transformed. A woman wearing a brightly coloured
dress had set up a fruit and flower stall. On it she had piled rows
of red apples alongside bunches of ripe, yellow bananas, orange
tangerines beside clusters of green grapes, and scarlet tomatoes
alongside amber pineapples. This fruit, together with the purples
and pinks and whites and maroons of Christmas chrysanthemums,
not only brought a splash of colour to brighten the drabness of
the day and the building, it also filled the air with fragrance.

Paul suggests that the life of the Christian should be equally
attractive, equally cheering and equally fragrant. He describes
the cluster of qualities that should characterise our lives:

Love
    joy
        peace
            patience
                kindness
                    goodness
                        faithfulness
                            gentleness
                                self-control

The reason why Jesus' personality and ministry were so magnetic was that in him each of these characteristics had been perfected. Towards God he was utterly loving. This love was demonstrated in his willingness to obey the Father in everything. His love for God and trust in him were so complete that his chief joy in life was his relationship with the Father. No matter what happened to him he remained unruffled, tranquil. Towards other people Jesus was kind, generous, reliable and forgiving. Indeed, such was his self-control that he never 'lost his cool'.

Paul places the spotlight on the attractiveness of this spiritual fruit for a particular reason – to plead with us to become like Jesus. There is only one way of ensuring that such spiritual produce germinates, grows and thrives in our lives – and that is to keep at the forefront of our minds the reminder that such spiritual produce is the fruit of the Holy Spirit. Without God's Spirit, these qualities cannot mature in us. *With* the root of the Spirit firmly embedded in us, though, the fruit will ripen, albeit over a period of time. As Jesus himself claims: 'Every good tree bears good fruit' (Matthew 7:17, NIV).

William Temple, author of *Basic Christianity*, explains why good trees bear good fruit and why it is essential for us to be indwelt with God's Spirit. It is useless, he insists, to give an ordinary person a play, such as *Hamlet* or *King Lear*, and expect them to be able to write a play like it. Shakespeare did it. Most people can't possibly imitate him. Similarly, it is no good showing us a life like Jesus' life and insisting that we should live our lives like that. Jesus could do it. We can't. If the genius of Shakespeare could invade us, though, we could then write plays like Shakespeare. Similarly, if the Spirit of Jesus dwells in us, we can, by the Spirit's grace, learn to live the Jesus life.

The good news is that the Spirit of Jesus *has* come. His equipping and empowering are available for those who ask:

> . . . God has given us the Holy Spirit, who fills our hearts with his love. (Romans 5:5, CEV)

Lent is often the season where we sense our need to make a fresh start with God by inviting the Holy Spirit to dwell in us afresh so that he can further transform us into the likeness of Jesus. Even when we have done this, such spiritual fruit ripens only slowly. That is why, this week, we ask God to increase his effectiveness in us as we look in detail at the kind of life he wants us to live.

Lord,
you examine me and know me,
you know if I am standing or sitting,
you read my thoughts from far away.
Whether I walk or lie down, you are watching,
you know every detail of my conduct . . .
Examine me and know my heart,
probe me and know my thoughts;
make sure I do not follow pernicious ways,
and guide me in the way that is everlasting.
(Psalm 139:1-3; 23, 24, JB)

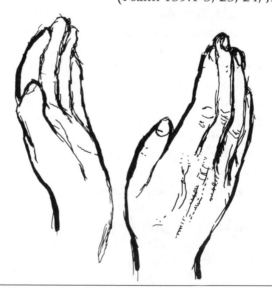

Day 20

# A Useful Thermometer

Self-examination is rather like taking your spiritual temperature. Paul's description of the harvest of the Spirit provides a useful thermometer for such purposes.

> The Spirit brings . . . love, joy, peace, patience, kindness, goodness, trustfulness, gentleness and self-control.
>
> (Galatians 5:22, 23, JB)

This week, we shall examine these gifts of the Spirit in an attempt to discover whether these manifestations of the Spirit's presence may be detected in our own life. This is one method of discerning some ways in which we can best make a fresh start with God and become more Christ-like in our behaviour and attitudes.

Today we focus on the Spirit's gift of gentleness. Whenever I think of the word 'gentleness' my mind goes back to the occasion when I was hospitalised in a country where few people spoke English. The reason why I was lying in this hospital with my head crowned with bandages was that I had sustained head and back injuries in a terrifying car crash. The elderly women who were my fellow patients in a primitive ward in what was then Yugoslavia were unable to communicate with me verbally, but each evening, before lights-out, they would come and gently kiss my forehead. These gentle gestures and the generosity with which they shared with me the food their relatives brought them comforted and strengthened me and gave me a sense of well-being in the middle of the trauma.

Another person who incarnated gentleness for me was the only doctor in the hospital who spoke a smattering of English. When he was off duty, he would come and sit at my bedside to talk to me – gently attempting to discover how our camping car had left the road and somersaulted down an embankment. When he heard the story, he was both angry with the lorry driver who had forced us off the road and concerned for my family and me.

The reason why I think of him when I hear the word 'gentleness' is because gentleness has been defined as the middle road between becoming too angry in the face of injustice and not being angry at all. In other words, a gentle person will be angry at the appropriate time and for the right reason but he or she will be so in control of their feelings that they will refrain from expressing anger at an inappropriate time or in an inappropriate way.

Those of a gentle spirit are those who are considerate, courteous and kind. Gentleness is a kindness which expresses itself in active service to meet the perceived needs of others. What is more, the gentle person is so concerned with the feelings and well-being of others that he or she will never cause needless hurt and will never resort to rudeness, abruptness or abrasiveness. Even when the gentle person has to be firm, this firmness will be laced with compassion, tenderness, and the self-control without which these qualities would be impossible.

*For the gentleness I have witnessed and received,*
*I thank you, Lord.*
*I covet this fruit of your Spirit for myself.*
*May it mature and mellow in me,*
*that I, too, may become increasingly gentle*
*in my dealings with others – those I know,*
*and the strangers whom I meet.*
*May my thoughts as well as my words*
*display this beautiful characteristic:*
*a gentle, Christ-like spirit.*

## Day 21

# Spiritual Fruit: Love

Just as a healthy vine will produce good grapes, so a Christian who is full of the Spirit's life will produce spiritual fruit. Paul claims that:

The fruit of the Spirit is love. (Galatians 5:22, NIV)

The love Paul mentions here is not love trivialised or love commercialised. On the contrary, it is Jesus' love: the unselfish affection and unceasing activity that seeks only the well-being of the loved one – the love that is born from the desire to meet the person's deepest needs and to promote his or her growth. This love is inextinguishable. No matter what a person may do to insult or injure or humiliate us, we will seek only his or her highest good. This dimension of love affects the mind and the will even more than the emotions. As Paul puts it:

Love is patient, love is kind. It does not envy, it does not boast, it is not proud. It is not rude, it is not self-seeking, it is not easily angered, it keeps no record of wrongs . . . It always protects, always trusts, always hopes, always perseveres. Love never fails.                    (1 Corinthians 13:4, 5, 7, 8, NIV)

The Greek word for love that is used here is *agape*. A person filled with agape love is someone who always seeks the best for another person even when that person hurts or insults them. Agape love offers tenderness and kindness to those not liked, to those who do not love the person who loves, and to the seemingly unlovable. Agape love refuses to harbour bitterness or seek revenge. It always seeks to promote the good of the person no matter what that person has done to them.

Our model for this kind of love-in-action is Jesus. Time after time his disciples let him down and failed to understand his mission. Nevertheless, as Jesus prepares to leave them he expresses unending love for them. This love is extended to all mankind and was supremely demonstrated in Jesus' death on Calvary:

God demonstrates his own love for us in this: While we are still sinners, Christ died for us.                    (Romans 5:8, NIV)

*Jesus,*
*I marvel at your healing, self-giving love.*
*When I am hurt,*
*neglected,*
*or when friends reject my love,*
*I withdraw –*
*cold, silent, prickly, bruised.*
*Yet your love never gives up.*
*You see the one you love*
*and think, not of your own needs,*
*but of the other's need to be restored and loved.*
*Teach me to give as you give;*
*to love as you love.*
*Produce in me a qualitative love –*
*that is always in season.*


Lord,
Grant that I may seek rather to comfort
than to be comforted;
to understand than to be understood;
to love than to be loved;
for it is by forgetting self that one finds;
it is by dying that one awakens to eternal life.

*From a prayer by St Francis of Assisi.*

## Day 22

# More Spiritual Fruit: Joy and Kindness

Mother Teresa of Calcutta, who dedicated her life to rescuing the deprived and dying, particularly in India's worst slums, radiated joy even when she was confronted with abject poverty, stench and intolerable need.

Paul reveals the source of that joy when he says:

What the Spirit brings is . . . joy. (Galatians 5:22, JB)

Joy is much more than a fleeting feeling. It is the ability to rejoice in spite of difficult places, difficult people or persistent pain. People who are filled with this kind of joy are those who have burrowed their roots into the soil of God's love. Mother Teresa underlined the importance of this fruit of God's Spirit when she claimed that:

- the best way we can show our gratitude to God and to others is by accepting everything with joy;
- those who give most are those who give with joy;
- joy is a net of love in which we can catch souls;
- a heart that burns with love gives birth to joy.

When the Holy Spirit is active in our lives, he also produces within us the fruit of kindness:

What the Spirit brings is . . . kindness. (Galatians 5:22, JB)

Mother Teresa had much to teach us about this fruit too. She urged us to become the living expression of God's kindness to the poor – to allow no one to come to us without coming away better and happier. If we are to incarnate God's kindness in this radical way, we must give our hearts as well as our care to children, to the vulnerable, to those who suffer, to the lonely and to the poor.

Lord,
my life is not always characterised by joy.
Sometimes clouds of despondency, disappointment
and dissatisfaction overshadow me –
like thunderclouds blotting out the rays of the sun.
There are times, too, when I don't want to be kind:
I even consider it my right to hate,
to point the finger and to withhold love.
May your Spirit enable me to make a fresh start
by changing me into your likeness –
even filling me with joy and kindness
until, like Jesus, I am constantly kind in a cruel world.

## Day 23

# Peace

The need for peace in the world is more urgent now than ever before. Peace starts in the heart of the individual and then spreads from one person to another. Mother Teresa explained how it could spread when she exhorted us to so radiate the peace of God and light God's light that peace and light would extinguish in the world and in people's hearts all hatred and love for power. Mother Teresa was simply building on the claims of Jesus and Paul.

Jesus said:

'Peace I bequeath to you, my own peace I give you.'
(John 14:27, JB)

Paul said:

The Spirit produces . . . peace. (Galatians 5:22, GNB)

The peace that is spoken of here is the ability to remain calm, tranquil and serene in all circumstances because we entrust our life and loved ones to the wisdom, sovereignty and protective care of God.

Peace is the quality of life that the Dutch Christian Betsie ten Boom demonstrated in the concentration camp at Ravensbruck. Although her father had been tortured and murdered and although she and her sister endured intolerable conditions in the camp, peace so controlled her that she was able to bring comfort and joy to the women who were fellow-prisoners with her. Peace so pervaded her spirit that she transformed the foul cell which she shared with crowds of other women. As her sister, Corrie ten Boom, recalled it, even in that cell, Betsie used her creative gift in such a way that the straw pallets were rolled instead of piled in a heap. Standing these up so that they looked like pillars along the walls, Betsie topped each with a lady's hat. She also managed to hang a headscarf along the wall, further transforming the drab and soulless cell into a place of comparative beauty. The contents of several food packages were also arranged on a small shelf and even the coats hanging on their hooks became part of the welcome of that room because Betsie draped each sleeve over the shoulder of the coat next to it so that the coats looked like a row of dancing children.

Peaceful people do not need to *speak* about Christ, they radiate his love and his likeness. As someone who had been a patient in a certain hospital wrote:

> For me, 'twas not the truth you taught
> to you so clear, to me so dim
> but when you came to me you brought
> a sense of him –
> and from your eyes he beckons me
> and from your heart his love is shed
> till I lose sight of you, and see
> the Christ instead.
>
> *Source unknown*
>
> *Father, fill me afresh with your Holy Spirit*
> *that people may watch the way I live and see,*
> *not me, but you shining through me.*

Peace, perfect peace, in this dark world of sin?
The blood of Jesus whispers peace within.

Peace, perfect peace, by thronging duties pressed?
To do the will of Jesus, this is rest.

Peace, perfect peace, our future all unknown?
Jesus we know, and he is on the throne.

Peace, perfect peace, death shadowing us and ours?
Jesus has vanquished death and all its powers.

It is enough: earth's struggles soon shall cease,
And Jesus calls us to heaven's perfect peace.

*Edward Henry Bickersteth (1825–1906)*

Show us, good Lord,
the peace we should seek,
the peace we must give,
the peace we can keep,
the peace we must forgo,
and the peace you have given in Jesus our Lord.

*Source unknown*

## Day 24

# Patience

There was once a Scottish school teacher who endeared himself to his pupils with his patience. Whenever a child submitted a piece of work that was ink-stained, this teacher would draw round the blob of ink and create from it an angel before handing the corrected piece of work back to the pupil concerned. This generous gesture encouraged many careless pupils to want to change.

Such acceptance of people's weaknesses does not come naturally to most of us. It is a quality of life, though, that Paul, in his letter to the Galatians, encourages us to acquire. He tells us that:

The fruit of the Spirit is . . . patience. (Galatians 5:22, NIV)

The patience mentioned here involves an endurance that refers chiefly to our relationships with people. This patience is the generosity a person displays when he or she could take revenge against someone who has injured or insulted or hurt them but who chooses not do to so. We see this kind of patience modelled for us most perfectly by Jesus:

[Jesus] was painfully abused,
    but he did not complain.
He was silent like a lamb
    being led to the butcher,
as quiet as a sheep
    having its wool cut off.
            (Isaiah 53:7, CEV)

Pilate asked him, 'Don't you hear what crimes they say you have done?' But Jesus did not say anything, and the governor was greatly amazed.
            (Matthew 27:13,14, CEV)

Jesus,
thank you for the example you have set me.
I want to learn to be as patient with others as you are with me.
Pour into my heart the spirit of tolerance,
acceptance and an unquenchable love for people.
When friends let me down,
or people fail to live up to my expectations,
keep me from withdrawing my affection;
enable me, instead, to go on loving and praying
and trying to understand.

## Day 25

# Be Filled with the Spirit

Corrie ten Boom, who became a world-famous speaker, teacher and author after her release from the Ravensbruck concentration camp, tells of an occasion when God transformed her attitude and behaviour. She was speaking at a meeting in Germany at the time. As she gave her talk, she noticed that one woman in the audience seemed unable to look Corrie in the eyes. After a while, Corrie realised that this woman was the nurse who had inflicted on Corrie's sister, Betsie, unimaginable cruelty. Corrie admits that when she recognised the nurse, memories of the way she had caused Betsie to suffer surfaced. Consequently, her heart was flooded with a bitterness that bordered on hatred.

Corrie knew that her duty as a Christian was to forgive this woman. She struggled, but she could not do it. 'Lord, you know I can't forgive her,' she whispered under her breath. 'My sister suffered too much because of her cruelties.'

At the suggestion of a friend, Corrie invited the nurse to attend the meeting the following night. The nurse came. During the entire meeting she looked steadily into Corrie's eyes as she spoke. When the meeting was over, Corrie had a talk with her. She told the nurse that, although she had felt full of bitterness, the Holy Spirit had replaced all that hatred with his love. Among other things, Corrie also told the nurse that she now loved her instead of hating her. As a result of this testimony to the grace of God, the nurse opened her own heart to the life-changing love of God.

Just as God, by his Spirit, changed Corrie ten Boom's bitterness into love, so he longs to cultivate within the life of each Christian the fruit of the Spirit which we have examined this week.

If this is to happen we, too, must open ourselves to the grace of God's Spirit. As Paul puts it, we must:

. . . be filled with the spirit. (Ephesians 5:18, NIV)

To enable us to make a similar Spirit-inspired, Spirit-enabled fresh start with God this Lent, there could be value in asking ourselves some searching questions:

Am I truly loving?
Am I joyful?
Am I a peaceful person?
Have I learned to exercise patience?
Do I express kindness, gentleness and goodness to those I live with and those I meet?
Am I self-controlled?

The reason for putting these questions to ourselves is not so that our many and frequent failures might swamp us but rather so that the Holy Spirit might reveal to us where we are making progress and which areas he would have us work on next. The Holy Spirit's work is to challenge us, to convict us and to enable us to change. When a person is willing to be changed, this third person of the Holy Trinity can effect remarkable transformations.

Receiving

You show me myself, Lord
and you show me where I need
to change and be changed.
I want to change, but I feel
powerless to do this alone.
May your life-transforming Spirit
fall on me afresh
and fill me anew.
I open myself to him and ask that,
little by little, I may change and be changed –
for your glory and my effectiveness.

## Week Five

# The Nature of God's Love

## Day 26

## Jesus' Love

Lent is a time for focusing on the mystery of God's love – a time to ponder it and to attempt to drink in the mystery of it all.

I once read a story which helps my heart to respond to that love. The story is of a young angel who was being shown round the splendours and glories of the universe by a more experienced angel.

The little angel was shown whirling galaxies and blazing suns, infinite distances in interstellar space and, finally, the galaxy of which our own planetary system is a part. As the two of them drew near to the star which we call our sun and to its circling planets, the senior angel pointed to Planet Earth. To the little angel, whose mind was still full of the grandeur and glory he had just seen, this planet looked as dull and dirty as a tennis ball.

'What's special about that one?' he asked.

'That,' replied his senior solemnly, 'is the Visited Planet. That ball, which to you looks so insignificant, has been visited by the Prince of Glory.'

'Do you mean to say,' queried the younger one, 'that our great and glorious Prince, with all these wonders and splendours of his creation, and millions more, which I'm sure I haven't seen yet, went down in person to this fifth-rate little ball? Why should he do a thing like that?'

'He did it because he loves the people there,' replied the senior angel. 'He went down to visit them so that he could lift them up to become like him.'

The little angel looked blank. Such thoughts were quite beyond his comprehension. Even so it is true. As John puts it in his Gospel:

God loved the world so much that he gave his only Son . . . to be the means by which our sins are forgiven.

(John 3:16; 1 John 4:10, GNB)

Philip Yancey sums up the mystery memorably in his book, *What's So Amazing About Grace?*, when he underlines the amazing fact that there is nothing we can do to make God love us more and there is nothing we can do to make God love us less. In other words, perfect, unbreakable love is what God is. His love is constant. It never grows tired and never gives up. To be in touch with God is to be in touch with love and to be held in it.

How precious it is, Lord,
to realise that you are thinking about me constantly!
I can't even count how many times a day
your thoughts turn towards me.
And when I wake in the morning,
you are still thinking of me!

(Psalm 139:17,18, LB)

O the deep, deep love of Jesus!
Vast, unmeasured, boundless, free;
rolling as a mighty ocean
in its fullness over me.
Underneath me, all around me,
is the current of thy love;
leading onward, leading homeward,
to thy glorious rest above.

*Samuel Trevor Francis (1834–1925)*

Day 27

# Drinking in God's Love

In the fourteenth century, there lived a woman of prayer who has come to be known as Julian of Norwich. One of her claims to fame is that she is believed to have been the first woman author in this country. She is best known, though, as a woman of prayer and a teacher of prayer. A message that she never tired of communicating was this: 'Love was God's meaning.' Today we focus on some of her sayings, so that we can drink in a small portion of God's love for *us*:

The best prayer is to rest in the goodness of God, knowing that that goodness can reach right down to our lowest depths of need.*

On one occasion God gave to Mother Julian a series of visions that deepened her love for Jesus:

I saw the red blood trickle down from under the garland, hot and fresh and plentiful, as it did at the time of his Passion when the crown of thorns was pressed into his blessed head – he who was both God and man and who suffered for me.

As I see it, God is all that is good, has made all that is made, and loves all he has made.*

* Julian of Norwich, *Enfolded in Love: Daily Readings with Julian of Norwich*, (Darton, Longman & Todd, London, 1980) p. 5.

Mother Julian was, of course, underlining the mind-blowing claim that was made by John when he wrote:

God loved the world so much that he gave his only Son, so that everyone who believes in him may not die but have eternal life.
(John 3:16, GNB)

One of the most powerful ways of drinking in the enormity of this love is to do the following:

Be silent,
be still.
Alone,
empty before your God.
Say nothing,
ask nothing.
Be silent.
Be still.
Let your God look upon you.
That is all.
God knows and understands.
God loves you with enormous love,
wanting only
to look upon you with love.
Quiet,
still,
be.

*Author unknown*

Day 28

# Suffering Love

It wasn't easy for Jesus to die for me. That realisation dawned on me when I was sitting by the Sea of Galilee at the beginning of Holy Week one year. I was meditating on some verses from Luke's Gospel at the time:

> Jesus took the twelve disciples aside and said to them, 'Listen! We are going to Jerusalem where everything the prophets wrote about the Son of Man will come true. He will be handed over to the Gentiles, who will mock him, insult him, and spit on him. They will whip him and kill him.'     (Luke 18:31-33, GNB)

How did Jesus feel when the time came for him to tear himself away from this tranquil place that he loved so much to go up to Jerusalem, knowing what would happen to him? That was the question I turned over and over in my mind as I watched the sun play on the calm, sparkling lake.

It was Palm Sunday and my husband and I were spinning out our last two hours in the sun before tearing ourselves away from Galilee and journeying to Jerusalem. I dreaded the thought of exchanging the warmth, the stillness and the beauty of the lakeside for the chill and bustle of the city. How much more heavy-hearted Jesus must have been when he turned *his* back on Galilee and set his face towards Calvary.

As we travelled to Jerusalem by bus later that day, I thought of the way Jesus had warned his disciples of his impending death. He knew that Jews and Gentiles alike would spit in his face, laugh him to scorn as though he were a buffoon, and hit him so hard with their clenched fists that their blows would cause him to double up with pain. He also knew that his scourged and flogged body would be strung up on a cross. Yet he went through with it. 'Why? Why? Why?' I kept asking myself and God.

Eventually, the answer came – loud, clear and brief:
It was love. Pure love.

St Paul writes:

> The Son of God who loved me and sacrificed himself for my sake. (Galatians 2:20, JB)

Or, as John Newton put it:

> Amazing grace! How sweet the sound
> that saved a wretch like me.
> I once was lost,
> but now I'm found;
> was blind, but now I see.

Day 29

# Rescuing Love

When God first created mankind, he intended that an intimate relationship should exist between the Creator and his creatures. The first man and woman, however, chose to live for self rather than for God. Through their disobedience, sin made its ugly entry into the world. God's people now walked in darkness, oppressed by Satan and alienated from God. Spiritually speaking, they lived in a never-ending winter. Enslaved by sin as they were, they were doomed to die both physically and spiritually:

> [Adam's] sin brought death with it. As a result, death has spread to the whole human race because everyone has sinned.
>
> (Romans 5:12, GNB)

C. S. Lewis provided us with perhaps the most powerful illustration of this that has ever been painted when he wrote his unforgettable allegory: *The Lion, the Witch and the Wardrobe*. Using the powerful medium of storytelling, he takes us into a world where it is always winter – into a land which is ruled by a White Witch. The owner of this land of Narnia, however, is Aslan – a handsome lion. As Aslan unexpectedly approaches Narnia, winter gives way to spring. The snow melts and spring flowers appear. Knowing that the arrival of spring is synonymous with the arrival of Aslan, the White Witch determines to kill the Lion. Aslan surrenders to her. With great jubilation, the White Witch butchers him to death. But her jubilation is shortlived. Within hours, Aslan springs back to life.

Between now and Easter, we shall focus on the way Jesus gave *himself* up. We shall observe how he was butchered to death. Today, though, we simply focus on the reason why he did it.

Jesus knew that there was only one solution to the problem of sin. He, the man-who-had-never-sinned, would need to take upon himself every sin each individual in the world had ever committed and would ever commit. As he carried these sins, it would be as though he himself had committed the crimes of the cosmos. He would therefore pay the penalty of sin in person. He knew what this penalty would be – the death penalty.

The hymn-writer, Cecil Frances Alexander, explains why he had to die:

He did it for me.

> We may not know, we cannot tell,
> what pains he had to bear;
> but we believe it was for us
> he hung and suffered there.
>
> There was no other good enough
> to pay the price of sin;
> he only could unlock the gate
> of heaven, and let us in.
>
> *C. F. Alexander (1818–1895)*
>
> *May that simple sentence,*
> *'He did it for me',*
> *prise open my mind and my heart,*
> *dear Jesus,*
> *as I journey with you to Jerusalem.*

## Day 30

# Crucified Love

> When I survey the wondrous Cross,
> on which the Prince of glory died,
> my richest gain I count but loss,
> and pour contempt on all my pride.
>
> *Isaac Watts (1674–1748)*

The composer of that well-loved hymn challenges us to not merely cast a cursory glance at the Cross, but to gaze at it reverently and with adoration. We can do that today by looking long and hard and lovingly at the picture of the crucifixion below. The nail-prints remind us that men split Jesus' hands and feet as they pinned him to the death gibbet. The pierced heart reminds us that his heart as well as his body was broken as he was hoisted on high for all to see – despised and mocked by those he had come to rescue.

Without beauty, without majesty (we saw him),
no looks to attract our eyes;
a thing despised and rejected by men,
a man of sorrows and familiar with suffering,
a man to make people screen their faces . . .
We thought of him as someone punished,
struck by God, and brought low.
Yet he was pierced through for our faults,
crushed for our sins.
On him lies a punishment that brings us peace,
and through his wounds we are healed.

(Isaiah 53:2-5, JB)

*May I drink in these profound truths,
dear Jesus:*

*mine were the sufferings you bore,
mine the sorrows you carried –
you were pierced through for my faults,
crushed because of my sin.*

*You did it for me.*

*God laid on you the punishment that brought me
peace, joy and a whole new start in life –
may my life become my
thank-you.*

## Day 31

# Forgiving Love

This picture reminds us of the pain that Jesus endured for our sake – how his body was scourged and flogged before the crude cross was loaded on to his torn and bleeding back. It reminds us, too, of the way he stumbled along the rough, cobbled streets of Jerusalem to the hill of Calvary.

As you gaze at this picture, ponder the psalm that follows. Some commentators believe that this foresees the cry of Jesus on the journey to Golgotha:

How much longer, Lord, will you forget about me?
Will it be for ever? How long will you hide?
How long must I be confused and miserable all day?
How long will my enemies keep beating me down?

Please listen, Lord God, and answer my prayers.
Make my eyes sparkle again,
or else I will fall into the sleep of death.
My enemies will say, 'Now we've won!'
They will be greatly pleased when I am defeated.
(Psalm 13:1-4, CEV)

Imagine how it might feel to touch the cruel crown of thorns that pierced his brow. Then listen to the cry of love which silences the swearing of the soldiers:

'Father, forgive them, for they do not know what they are doing.'
(Luke 23:33, JB)

What a prayer to pray over your persecutors! Jesus prayed it because, even in this hour of physical torture, what he most wanted was that his tormentors and you and I should enjoy the peace with God he was purchasing for us on the Cross.

See from his head, his hands, his feet,
sorrow and love flow mingled down;
did e'er such love and sorrow meet,
or thorns compose so rich a crown?

*Isaac Watts (1674–1748)*

Love and sorrow had never before merged in this way. Neither had thorns ever created such a magnificent crown. Never before had God hung on a tree.

O sacred head, surrounded
by crown of piercing thorn!
O bleeding head, so wounded,
so shamed and put to scorn!
Death's pallid hue comes o'er thee,
the glow of life decays;
yet angel-hosts adore thee,
and tremble as they gaze.

*P. Gerhardt*
based on *Salve caput cruentatum*
trans. Sir H. W. Baker

# Day 32

# Beckoning Love

The love of Jesus, which beckons us from the Cross, demands a response:

> Every advantage that I had gained I considered lost for Christ's sake. Yes, and I look upon everything as loss compared with the overwhelming gain of knowing Christ Jesus my Lord.
>
> (Philippians 3:7-9, JBP)

A man called Ron once told me why *he* boasts about Christ's Cross. Ron was a paratrooper in the Second World War. On New Year's Eve, 1944, his battalion stayed in an abbey in France. Just before he left the abbey, one of the monks gave Ron a metal crucifix.

On the morning of 24 March 1945, as he rushed for reveille, Ron stuffed this crucifix into his battledress pocket. He was unaware as he did so that his battalion would be crossing the Rhine that day by plane and that he would be commanded to jump from the plane. Ron *did* jump. As he landed, his parachute was punctured by a burst of enemy bullets and his body was spun round by the force of the fire. Mercifully, he was able to run, unhurt, to a trench where he took shelter. There, in the trench, he discovered that his smock, battledress and shirt were peppered with bullet holes. Two days later, having staggered to a military hospital, he stripped off his clothes so that he could have a bath. As he removed his soiled clothing, he discovered why he had escaped injury. Embedded in his clothes he found the spent bullet that

75

had torn them. He also drew out of his pocket the metal crucifix, which was now broken in two. As he gazed at it, the truth dawned: this cross had taken the full impact of the bullet and had protected his body from being punctured like his parachute. The cross, quite literally, had saved his life.

This happened nearly sixty years ago. Every day, from that day to this, Ron has thanked God for a life which might have ended in 1945.

One way in which we can make a fresh start with God is by becoming equally aware of, and grateful for, the fact that a cross has also saved our lives. As the hymn writer Isaac Watts reminds us, our lives were saved by the sacrifice Jesus made for us by hanging on the cruel Cross of Calvary. Ponder Isaac Watts' words which sum up the mystery of Christ's 'wondrous Cross'. Echo the words if you feel you can:

> Forbid it, Lord, that I should boast,
> save in the Cross of Christ my God;
> all the vain things that charm me most,
> I sacrifice them to his blood . . .
>
> Were the whole realm of nature mine
> that were an offering far too small;
> love so amazing, so divine,
> demands my soul, my life, my all.
>
> *Isaac Watts (1674–1748)*

## Week Six

# What Christ's Death Achieved

## Day 33

## Ransomed

This week, we focus on what Christ's death on the Cross achieved. A true story of self-sacrificing love helps me to catch a glimpse of its effectiveness.

A man I know was once caught stealing from his employers. When the court case was heard, the judge imposed a fine of £50. Failure to pay the prescribed fine, he threatened, would result in imprisonment.

The night of the court hearing, the guilty one despaired. He had no money. That was why he had resorted to stealing in the first place. How was he to pay the fine? The thought of a period in prison filled him with shame and dread.

Next morning, to his amazement, a brown envelope dropped through his letterbox. On opening it, he discovered ten new, crisp, five-pound notes and a handwritten explanation: 'To pay off the debt'.

The offender never discovered where the money had come from. The only information he could glean was that members of a nearby church had heard of his plight and resolved to set him free from the threat of imprisonment.

When Jesus died on the cruel Cross, he bought our release from the clutches of the Evil One. He also set us free from the bondage to sin in which we had been trapped all our lives. He delivered us, too, from the effects of our sin-stained past and from the guilt that enshrouded us:

Everyone was going to be punished because Adam sinned. But because of the good thing that Christ has done, God accepts us and gives us the gift of life. (Romans 5:18, CEV)

God loved the people of this world so much that he gave his only Son, so that everyone who has faith in him will have eternal life and never really die. (John 3:16, CEV)

The only thing that is required of us is that we accept this free and perfect gift. As one hymn-writer sums up the miracle:

> Inscribed upon the Cross we see
> in shining letters, 'God is Love':
> he bears our sins upon the tree;
> he brings us mercy from above.
>
> The Cross! It takes our guilt away;
> it holds the fainting spirit up;
> it cheers with hope the gloomy day,
> and sweetens every bitter cup.
>
> *Thomas Kelly (1769–1854)*

---

From the deep places of my soul,
I praise you, O God:
I lift up my heart and glorify your holy name.
From the deep places of my soul,
I praise you, O God:
how can I forget all your goodness towards me?
You forgive all my sin,
you heal all my weaknesses,
you rescue me from the brink of disaster,
you crown me with mercy and compassion . . .
For you have triumphed over the power of death,
and draw us to your presence with songs of joy . . .
From the widest bounds of the universe
to the depths of my very being,
the whispers and cries of joy
vibrate to a shining glory,
O God, our beginning and our end.

*Jim Cotter*

## Day 34

# Healed

The words: 'I love you' are among the most healing we can ever say to anyone if we really mean what we are saying. We all need to know that we are uniquely loved.

The Uttered Word,
On Calvary so
silenced by our
sins,
Today is heard
In new, eternal
triumph-song:

"LOVE WINS"

For this and many other reasons, Jesus' sacrificial death on the Cross brings healing to many hurting people because it conveys, more effectively than any words, the fact that he loves us. As Paul put it in his letter to the Romans:

No one is really willing to die for an honest person, though someone might be willing to die for a truly good person. But God showed how much he loved us by having Christ die for us, even though we were sinful.

(Romans 5:7-8, CEV)

Christians know that God loves them because the historical fact of Jesus' death provides them with objective proof of this amazing good news.

As though that gift of love was insufficient proof of his love, God provides us with yet more evidence that his love for us is intimate. Paul put it this way:

. . . God has given us the Holy Spirit, who fills our hearts with his love. (Romans 5:5, CEV)

In other words, God's healing love is to be felt as well as to be absorbed with the mind. Revd John Stott, author, teacher and founder of the London Institute for Christianity, believes this so passionately that he encourages us to gaze at Christ's Cross and to drink in this amazing proof of his love. He begs us to turn our gazing into a request that God would flood our hearts, not only with his love but with his Spirit also. Then, he urges us to allow any fears we may have to be swallowed up in God's steadfast love.

Thanks be to you,
our Lord Jesus Christ,
for all the benefits which you have given us,
for all the pains and insults
which you have borne for us.
Most merciful Redeemer, Friend and Brother,
may we know you more clearly,
love you more dearly,
and follow you more nearly,
day by day.

*Prayer of St Richard*

## Day 35

# Restored

When the mother of two toddlers was admitted to hospital prior to the birth of her third child, her doctor examined her and predicted a normal delivery and a big, bouncing baby. That night, the woman gave birth, but the labour was both prolonged and painful. Consequently, she was sedated heavily.

Next morning, the mother was shocked to learn that the baby was dead: stillborn, she was told. The hospital staff sympathised with her in her bereavement but advised her to return home and enjoy her other two children. Grief-stricken, the young woman left hospital and for nine months mourned the loss of the child she had wanted so much.

After these nine months, detectives knocked at the door of the woman's home and asked her to accompany them to a certain house bringing her other children with her. At the house, the woman saw a little girl, about nine months old, playing happily. Intuitively, this young woman knew that the child was *her* child. She opened her arms, caught up the little girl and cuddled her eagerly and lovingly.

The detectives smiled, observed the striking likeness between the baby and the woman's other children, and then explained the mystery. The child in her arms was, indeed, her child. While she had been under sedation after her delivery, a psychiatric patient had crept into the ward and had exchanged her stillborn baby for this woman's healthy child. For the past nine months this woman had brought up the child as though she were her own.

Through a mysterious sequence of events, the deceit had at last been uncovered. So the delighted, rightful mother was allowed to take her baby home knowing that, now her baby had been restored to her, their relationship could begin.

When Jesus gave his life for us at Calvary, what happened was that we were restored to a right relationship with God. Intimacy with him became a possibility once more. We were even accepted into God's family circle. As Paul expresses the mystery:

Let us grasp the fact that we *have* peace with God through our Lord Jesus Christ. Through him we have confidently entered into this new relationship of grace, and here we take our stand, in happy certainty of the glorious things he has for us in the future. (Romans 5:1, JBP)

You have been adopted into the very family circle of God and you can say with a full heart, 'Father, my Father'. The Spirit himself endorses our inward conviction that we really are the children of God. Think what that means. If we are his children we share his treasures, and all that Christ claims as his will belong to all of us as well! (Romans 8:14, JBP)

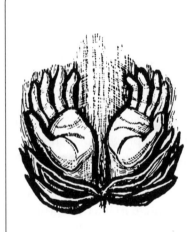

Eternal Light,
shine into our hearts;
Eternal Goodness,
deliver us from evil;
Eternal Power, be our support;
Eternal Wisdom, scatter the
darkness of our ignorance;
Eternal Pity, have mercy on us;
that with all our heart and
soul and mind and strength
we may seek your face and be
brought by your infinite mercy
to your holy presence;
through Jesus Christ our Lord.

*Alcuin (c. 732–804)*

## Day 36

# Forgiven

'To forgive' does not mean 'to forget', 'to excuse', 'to pretend it never happened'. The Greek word for 'to forgive' is *aphesis*, which means 'to drop', 'to let go of', 'to relinquish'.

In other words, when Jesus cried his heart-rending prayer from the Cross, 'Father forgive', he was not begging his Father to *forget* the sin of the world, neither was he, himself, seeking to forget that he was encircled by many who wished him only harm. What he was doing was carrying the burden of the sin of the whole world and suffering – then dying – instead of us. In other words, because of Jesus' death at Calvary, *we* can know the joy of being on the receiving end of deep, lasting, real forgiveness.

Paul puts it powerfully in his letter to the Colossians:

God has now made you share in the very life of Christ! He has forgiven you all your sins: Christ has utterly wiped out the damning evidence of broken laws and commandments which always hung over our heads, and has completely annulled it by nailing it over his own head on the Cross. And then, having drawn the sting of all the powers ranged against us, he exposed them, shattered, empty and defeated, in his final glorious, triumphant act! (Colossians 2:13-15, JBP)

No one has put the situation more simply or powerfully than Cecil Francis Alexander in a hymn we sometimes mistakenly call a children's hymn:

There is a green hill far away,
without a city wall,
where the dear Lord was crucified,
who died to save us all.

We may not know, we cannot tell,
what pains he had to bear;
but we believe it was for us
he hung and suffered there.

He died that we might be forgiven,
he died to make us good,
that we might go at last to heaven,
saved by his precious blood.

There was no other good enough
to pay the price of sin;
he only could unlock the gate
of heaven, and let us in.

O dearly, dearly has he loved,
and we must love him too,
and trust in his redeeming blood,
and try his works to do.

*Cecil Francis Alexander (1818–1895)*

Day 37

# Cleansed

The blood of Jesus is the best detergent in the world. When we apply it to our mistakes and failures, even our deliberate sins, it erases the stain completely and leaves us free to live before God and before others as though we had never ever sinned. God gave us this reminder through Isaiah when he said:

> I, the Lord, invite you
>     to come and talk it over.
> Your sins are scarlet red,
> but they will be whiter
>     than snow or wool.
>             (Isaiah 1:18, CEV)

As James Borst has expressed it in his book, *Coming to God*, we face God as chronic patients, being sinful and spiritually handicapped in so many ways. Because God accepts our handicaps and disabilities, we can also. He accepts us and loves us as we are. Rather than nurse a sense of guilt, we must fully and completely accept and embrace his forgiveness and love, surrendering everything to him and to his mercy.

When we do this, we can rejoice in the way the psalmist describes when he writes:

> What happiness for those whose guilt has been forgiven! What joys when sins are covered over! What relief for those who have confessed their sins and God has cleared their record.
>             (Psalm 32:1, 2, LB)

Lord, what joy you give me.
I come to you penitent,
crying over my sin.
You come to me
offering unlimited forgiveness,
sufficient grace to cancel all my guilt.
For a love that witnessed the full horror of my failure
and yet that goes on caring and forgiving,
I thank you
and rejoice from the depths of my being.

## Day 38

# Released

The death of Jesus not only cancels our sin-stained past. It does even more than this because it also deals with the guilt. Paul puts it this way:

> If God is for us, who can be against us? He that did not hesitate to spare his own Son but gave him up for us all – can we not trust such a God to give us, with him, everything else that we need? (Romans 8:32, 33, JBP)

A guilty person often lives with the dread that their past misdemeanours will be discovered. The guilty person, therefore, often becomes an anxious person – experiencing a continual inner conflict. But all this can change, because the death of Jesus is capable of dealing with our guilt.

An elderly lady I once met testified to this fact as she told me her story. She had lived 'a terrible life', she said. Aware that she was growing old, she decided that she would now like to live near her grandchildren. 'But', she reasoned, 'my daughter knows the kind of life I've led. Maybe she wouldn't want her mother so near? After all, I could influence her children, couldn't I?'

One day she told her daughter what was on her mind and her daughter's response took her by surprise: 'Why don't you put your trust in Jesus, Mummy? He can wipe out the past, set you free from it, and give you a completely new start.'

'At first, I hardly dared believe what she told me,' the old lady said. 'But I thought it was worth a try. So I told God I was sorry for the past. I asked him to forgive me. And d'you know what happened? He forgave me. He set me free from all that filth and evil. *Even the guilt has gone.* I didn't realise it was possible to be so happy. He's given me such joy. And I don't deserve it after what I've done.'

O make me understand it,
help me to take it in,
what it meant to thee, the Holy One,
to bear away my sin.

*Katherine A. M. Kelly (1869–1942)*

## Day 39

# Saved

We end this week as we began – with a true story which illustrates what Jesus' death on the Cross achieved. The story is of Natalie, a Russian woman of whom little is known except her name and the fact that she lived in Russia when civil war ravaged that country.

As war swept through the land, the wife of an officer in the White Army knew that it was imperative that she and her children should hide because the city where she lived had fallen into the hands of the Red Army. She hid in a small, wooden cabin on the outskirts of the city.

Towards evening on her second day in hiding, she heard a knock on the cabin door. On the doorstep stood a young woman of her own age. The woman, Natalie, spoke in whispers but urged the mother to leave that night, together with her children. 'You've been discovered,' she said. 'Tonight they will come.'

The mother looked down at her two small children. How could she escape? They would quickly be caught.

'Don't worry about the children. I'll stay here. They won't even look for you,' Natalie promised.

That night, Natalie came back. The mother and her two small boys escaped into the woods. Natalie faced the certainty of death alone. With the cold of morning the soldiers came. They battered down the door and, without checking her identity, shot her just where she was. Next day, she was found by friends – dead.

Natalie could have escaped from that cabin at any time. She chose not to. She died so that others might live.

Almost two thousand years before, a man of Natalie's age – Jesus – rode into Jerusalem to do something similar for us. He took upon himself all the guilt and horror of our sin. He suffered the whole weight of the judgement that was due to us. He sacrificed his own life so that ours might be saved.

> All of us were like sheep
>     that had wandered off.
> We had each gone our own way,
> but the Lord gave him
>     the punishment we deserved.
>                 (Isaiah 53:6, CEV)

> Were the whole realm of nature mine,
> that were an offering far too small;
> love so amazing, so divine,
> demands my soul, my life, my all.
>                 *Isaac Watts (1674–1748)*

# The Last Week of Jesus' Life

## Day 40

## Christ Triumphant

This week, Holy Week, we examine some of the events of the last week of Jesus' life and seek to understand what it cost him to go to the gallows.

As he was getting near Bethphage and Bethany on the Mount of Olives, he sent two of his disciples on ahead. He told them, 'Go into the next village, where you will find a young donkey that has never been ridden. Untie the donkey and bring it here. If anyone asks why you are doing that, just say, "The Lord needs it."'

They went off and found everything just as Jesus had said. While they were untying the donkey, its owners asked, 'Why are you doing that?'

They answered, 'The Lord needs it.'

Then they led the donkey to Jesus. They put some of their clothes on its back and helped Jesus get on. And as he rode along, the people spread clothes on the road in front of him. When Jesus was setting off down the Mount of Olives, his large crowd of disciples were happy and praised God because of all the miracles they had seen.

They shouted,

'Blessed is the king who comes
in the name of the Lord!
Peace in heaven and glory to God.'   (Luke 19:29-38, CEV)

Jesus knew when he entered Jerusalem with such a flourish that he was taking a double risk: the risk of rejection and the risk of death. He knew that there was a price on his head; that the religious leaders had laid traps for him. He knew, too, that in asking the question: 'Will you take me as your King?' he was inviting the reaction of the majority which would be an unequivocal 'No.'

O Lord, the house of my soul is narrow;
enlarge it, that you may enter in.
It is ruinous, O repair it!
It displeases your sight: I confess it, I know.
But who shall cleanse it, to whom shall I cry but to you?
Cleanse me from my secret faults, O Lord,
and spare your servant from strange sins.

*Augustine of Hippo (354–430)*

Day 41

# Jesus Cleanses the Temple

If the manner of Jesus' entry into Jerusalem was both courageous and defiant in the light of the fact that he was a marked man, his cleansing of the Temple on the Monday of Holy Week was even more daring. Mark tells the story vividly:

> On reaching Jerusalem, Jesus entered the temple area and began driving out those who were buying and selling there. He overturned the tables of the money changers and the benches of those selling doves, and would not allow anyone to carry merchandise through the temple courts. And as he taught them he said, 'Is it not written: "My house will be called a house of prayer for all the nations"? But you have made it "a den of robbers."' (Mark 11:15-17, NIV)

The Temple had been built as a house of prayer for all nations. Gentiles, though, were only allowed in one outer court, which the Jews abused by using it as a thoroughfare and for trade. Consequently it had also become a place for double-dealings. This outraged Jesus.

The money changers whose booths dominated these outer precincts of the Temple fleeced pilgrims by placing a heavy surcharge on every transaction they made. Similarly, the dove-sellers were equally deceitful. They charged extortionate prices for their wares and rejected any doves bought elsewhere, claiming that these were blemished and were therefore unfit offerings for God. With a ruthlessness that must have astonished all his onlookers, Jesus rid the Temple of these practices that could never coexist with a holy God.

Lord,
your word reminds me that I, too, am a temple;
that your Spirit has taken up residence inside me.
This Holy Week, reveal to me
those changes you would like to make in my life.
Put your finger on behaviour patterns,
attitudes and failures of mine
which cannot coexist with your Spirit.
Then give me, I pray,
the courage to deal ruthlessly with them –
before Easter Day dawns.

# Day 42

# The Betrayal

During Holy Week, Jesus suffered the pain of rejection, not simply from the religious leaders of the day, nor just from the crowds who thronged the streets of Jerusalem. Even his own disciples failed to understand his mission and, by their actions, added to his pain. Luke places the spotlight on Judas and shows how he colluded with the enemies of Jesus:

> Now as the feast of unleavened bread, called the Passover, was approaching, fear of the people made the chief priests and scribes try desperately to find a way of getting rid of Jesus. Then a diabolical plan came into the mind of Judas Iscariot, who was one of the twelve. He went and discussed with the chief priests and officers a method of getting Jesus into their hands. They were delighted and arranged to pay him for it. He agreed, and began to look for a suitable opportunity for betrayal when there was no crowd present. (Luke 22:1-5)*

It was the ambition of every Jew in the world to be present in Jerusalem at Passover time at least once in his lifetime. Because of this, vast numbers of people flocked to the holy city for the festival. The atmosphere was always inflammable. The Jewish authorities knew this and determined to arrest Jesus before the feast and therefore avoid a riot. Judas played right into their hands, offering to lead them to Jesus at an appropriate time and an appropriate place.

Judas was not the only disciple to fail his master during the last hours of Jesus' earthly ministry, however. Jesus knew that, when he needed his support most, even Peter would turn deserter. He warned Peter of this:

---

* J. B. Phillips, *The Gospels: Translated into Modern English* (Geoffrey Bles, London, 1952), p. 176.

Simon Peter said to him, 'Lord, where are you going?'

'I am going,' replied Jesus, 'where you cannot follow me now, though you will follow me later.'

'Lord, why can't I follow you now?' said Peter. 'I would lay down my life for you!'

'Would you lay down your life for me?' replied Jesus. 'Believe me, you will disown me three times before cockcrow!'

(John 13:36-38)*

Before the first Good Friday had dawned, each of Jesus' disciples had abandoned him to his fate. Matthew records the sad fact that after Jesus' arrest:

All the disciples left him and made their escape.*
(Matthew 26:56)

---

* J. B. Phillips, *The Gospels: Translated into Modern English* (Geoffrey Bles, London, 1952), pp. 223 and 60 respectively.

In the Book of Lamentations, we read a poem that is thought by some to predict the sufferings Jesus endured during this last week of his life:

Is it nothing to you, all you who pass by?
Look around and see.
Is any suffering like my suffering
that was inflicted on me?
. . . This is why I weep
and my eyes overflow with tears.
No one is near to comfort me,
no one to restore my spirit . . .
People have heard my groaning,
but there is no one to comfort me.
All my enemies have heard of my distress;
they rejoice at what you have done.
(Lamentations 1:12,16, 21, NIV)

O Lord our God,
grant us your grace
to desire you with our whole heart,
that so desiring we may seek and find you,
and so finding you, may love you,
and loving you, may hate those sins
from which you have redeemed us.

*(Anselm 1033–1109)*

Day 43

# The Last Supper

Just as Christians celebrate the birth of Jesus at Christmas time, so, at Passover time, the Jews celebrate the occasion when God delivered their nation from Egypt, where they had been enslaved. The Passover feast was one of the highlights of the year and Jesus longed to share this special meal with his closest friends, his disciples.

The disciples were never to forget this particular occasion, partly because it was to prove to be the last meal they would eat with Jesus before his death and partly because of the things Jesus did on this occasion. John describes one of the surprises Jesus sprung on that particular evening:

Jesus . . . rose from the supper table, took off his outer clothes, picked up a towel and fastened it around his waist. Then he poured water into the basin and began to wash the disciples' feet and to dry them with the towel around his waist . . . When Jesus had washed their feet and put on his clothes, he sat down again and spoke to them: 'Do you realise what I have just done to you? You call me "teacher" and "Lord" and are quite right, for I am your teacher and your Lord. But if I, your teacher and Lord, have washed your feet, you must be ready to wash one another's feet. I have given you this example so that you may do as I have done.'          (John 13:4-15)

In washing his friends' feet, Jesus had performed the most menial task imaginable. His challenge to us is: 'Love one another as I have loved you.'

Like every host at this particular meal, Jesus took bread and distributed it to his friends. Then he took a cup of wine and blessed it. Luke reminds us, though, that the words Jesus used on this occasion were unique.

And he took bread, gave thanks and broke it, and gave it to them, saying, 'This is my body given for you; do this in remembrance of me.' In the same way, after the supper he took the cup, saying, 'This cup is the new covenant in my blood, which is poured out for you.' (Luke 22:19, 20, NIV)

Jesus knew what the disciples did not yet know, that on the very next day, his body would literally be broken and his blood spilled. He was about to sacrifice his life as a once-and-for-all offering for sin. It was to be a kind of charter, sealed with his own blood, which would dwarf any other previous attempts to bring God and man together. *This* agreement, steeped as it was in sacrifice, would reconcile God and man for ever. *This* agreement would secure man's forgiveness from sin. *This* agreement proved that God's love for mankind was unquenchable.

Give us, O Lord God,
a deep sense of your wonderful love towards us;
how you would not let us alone in our ruin,
but came after us,
in the person of your Son Jesus Christ
to bring us back to our true home with you.
Quicken in us, O Lord,
the spirit of gratitude, of loyalty and of sacrifice,
that we may seek in all things to please him
who humbled himself for us,
even to the death of the Cross,
by dying to sin and living to righteousness;
through the same Jesus Christ our Lord.

*Charles J. Vaughan (1816–1879)*

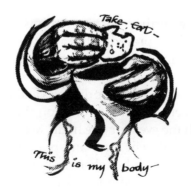

## Day 44

# The Garden of Gethsemane

On several occasions I have knelt in the Garden of Gethsemane and tried to imagine how Jesus might have felt on the night before he died. No one can even hope, though, to identify fully with the anguish the Son of God must have suffered as he pleaded with his Father to show him an escape route from the cross of Calvary. The Gospel writers do, however, give us a glimpse of some of the pain and turmoil which caused Jesus to plead with the Father to deliver him from the necessity of dying the death of a criminal. Matthew records some of Jesus' feelings:

> Then Jesus went with his disciples to a place called Gethsemane, and he said to them, 'Sit here while I go over there and pray.' He took with him Peter and the two sons of Zebedee. Grief and anguish came over him, and he said to them, 'The sorrow in my heart is so great that it almost crushes me. Stay here and keep watch with me.' (Matthew 26:36-38, GNB)

Matthew goes on to reveal the struggle Jesus had to accept the task which lay before him: that of bearing the loathsome burden of our sin in his own body on the Cross:

> He went a little further on, threw himself face downwards on the ground, and prayed, 'My Father, if it is possible, take this cup of suffering from me! Yet not what I want, but what you want.'
> Then he returned to the three disciples and found them asleep; and he said to Peter, 'How is it that you three were not able to keep watch with me even for one hour? Keep watch and pray . . .'
> Once more Jesus went away and prayed, 'My Father, if this cup of suffering cannot be taken away unless I drink it, your will be done.' He returned once more and found the disciples asleep; they could not keep their eyes open.
> (Matthew 26:39-43, GNB)

Luke describes even more graphically the agony Jesus encountered while he prayed:

> In great anguish he prayed . . . his sweat was like drops of blood falling to the ground. (Luke 22:44, GNB)

The Son of God gripped by fear!
The Son of God crushed by a killing sorrow!
The Son of God in anguish!
The Son of God sweating great drops of blood!
The Son of God shuddering in the face of death!
The Son of God shrinking at the cost of the Cross!

It was not easy for Jesus to die for me.

As William Barclay once put it, Jesus did not want to die. He was thirty-three years old and no one wants to die when the best years of life are just opening up. Yet, out of obedience to his Father, he compelled himself to go on.

As we watch Jesus at prayer in the garden, we see both the extent of his anguish and the strength the Spirit poured into him when he said 'Yes' to the Father's will.

It is a thing most wonderful,
almost too wonderful to be,
that God's own Son should come
    from heaven,
and die to save a child like me.

And yet I know that it is true;
he chose a poor and humble lot,
and wept, and toiled, and mourned,
    and died
for love of those who loved him not.

I sometimes think about the Cross,
and shut my eyes, and try to see
the cruel nails, and crown of thorns,
and Jesus crucified for me.

But even could I see him die,
I could but see a little part
of that great love, which, like a fire,
is always burning in his heart.

It is most wonderful to know
his love for me so free and sure;
but 'tis more wonderful to see
my love for him so faint and poor.

And yet I want to love thee, Lord;
O light the flame within my heart,
and I will love thee more and more,
until I see thee as thou art.

*William Walsham How (1823–1897)*

Day 45

# Good Friday

# Jesus is Crucified

Judas went through with his plan. He knew Jesus well enough to suspect that it would be to the Garden of Gethsemane that he would retreat. It was there he betrayed his master with a traitor's kiss. Throughout Thursday night, Jesus stood trial. Pilate, the Roman governor, could find no cause for imposing the death penalty, yet when he presented Jesus to the crowd, he capitulated to their clamour when they cried with one voice: 'Crucify him!'

The soldiers assigned to the governor took Jesus into the governor's palace and got the entire brigade together for some fun. They stripped him and dressed him in a red toga. They plaited a crown from branches of a thorn bush and set it on his head. They put a stick in his right hand for a sceptre. Then they knelt before him in mocking reverence: 'Bravo, King of the Jews!' they said. 'Bravo!' Then they spat on him and hit him on the head with the stick. When they had had their fun, they took off the toga and put his own clothes back on him. Then they proceeded out to the crucifixion.

(Matthew 27:27-32, The Message)

A huge crowd of people followed him, including women who wrung their hands and wept for him . . . Two criminals were also led out with him for execution, and when they came to the place called The Skull, they crucified him with the criminals, one on either side of him . . . (Luke 23:27-33)

It was now about midday, but darkness came over the whole countryside until three in the afternoon, for there was an eclipse of the sun. The veil in the Temple sanctuary was split in two. Then Jesus gave a great cry and said, 'Father, I commend my spirit into your hands.' And with these words he died.

(Luke 23:44-46, JBP)

They hammered nails through his hands and into the cross-beam. The nails split his feet as they cut into the cruel cross. They hoisted him, helpless, between two thieves. They flogged him and mocked him – then watched him die.

With John and Mary, we watch and marvel because:

Today he who hung the earth upon the waters
now hangs on a cruel cross.
He who is King of the angels now wears a crown of thorns.
He who wraps the heaven in clouds
is wrapped in the purple of mockery.
He who came to set mankind free
receives blow after blow on his face and body.
The Bridegroom of the Church is transfixed with nails. *

We worship you, Lord Jesus, as we reflect
on the mystery that it was neither the nails
nor the hatred of men that pinned you to the Cross,
it was LOVE. †

Draw us, we pray, ever closer to yourself.
Persuade us to ponder the claim
that if we love any ground more than the ground
at the foot of your Cross
we know nothing of Calvary love. §

* Inspired by a Good Friday hymn from the Orthodox Tradition.
† An observation originally penned by Elizabeth of the Trinity.
§ A claim once made by Amy Carmichael.

## Day 46

# Easter Saturday

# The Disciples Wait

Easter Saturday (or Holy Saturday as many Christians prefer to call it) can make a profound impact on us as we prepare to celebrate Easter Day. One way of ensuring that this happens is to earmark time on this day to seek to identify with the feelings that almost certainly consumed the first followers of Jesus on the day after Christ's crucifixion.

What did they do on that Saturday? Did they sit huddled behind locked doors for fear of recrimination from Jesus' enemies? Did they weep and mourn as they relived the last agonising moments of Jesus' life? Did they give voice to the pain that separation from their master must have inflicted on them? Were they restless or frustrated because they could not visit the scene of Jesus' burial earlier? Did they suffer that intolerable emptiness and numbness the bereaved person experiences when they have lost a loved one? Did they recall, even discuss, the way Jesus had washed their feet before the Last Supper? Did they talk about that memorable meal they had shared with him?

We are not told, but we may safely surmise that much of their day was spent remembering that unforgettable meal as well as reliving the horror of Gethsemane and Good Friday.

As we continue to focus on the events of Good Friday, we have the privilege of drinking in mysteries which the disciples were unaware of on the first Holy Saturday. As Peter was later to put it in one of his letters:

> [Jesus] was bearing our faults in his own body on the cross, so that we might die to our faults and live for holiness; through his wounds you have been healed. You had gone astray like sheep but now you have come back to the shepherd and guardian of your souls. (1 Peter 2:24, JB)

Peter's profound observation leaves us with a challenge which helps us to prepare to celebrate the resurrection of Jesus. The challenge lies embedded in the reminder that Jesus bore our faults in his body on the tree so that we might die to these faults and live, instead, for holiness – in other words, so that we might become Christlike.

Is this why some Christians spend this day reflecting on questions such as:

- Do I renounce evil?
- Do I repent of the sin that separates me from God and from others?
- Do I return afresh to Jesus?

As we ask ourselves these questions today, perhaps we can liken ourselves to the women who spent part of this day preparing spices with which they would embalm the body of Jesus as soon as the Sabbath was over – the same women who, according to Luke, went to the tomb at the first sign of dawn, taking these aromatic spices with them (Luke 24:1).

*On the night before you died, dear Jesus,*
*you washed your disciples' feet.*
*On the day you died,*
*you became the Saviour of the world.*
*On this day, give me the grace*
*to remember with gratitude that you died for me.*
*May the memory so rekindle my love for you*
*so that, as Easter Day dawns,*
*I may dedicate myself to you afresh.*

Day 47

## Easter Day

# Christ is Risen! Hallelujah!

This good news reverberates around the world today just as joyfully as it was spread from disciple to disciple on that first Easter morning. John captures some of the awe, bewilderment and excitement which characterised this Day of Days:

Early on Sunday morning, while it was still dark, Mary Magdalene went to the tomb and saw that the stone had been taken away from the entrance . . . [She] stood crying outside the tomb. While she was still crying, she bent over and looked in the tomb and saw two angels there dressed in white, sitting where the body of Jesus had been, one at the head and the other at the feet. 'Woman, why are you crying?' they asked her.

She answered, 'They have taken my Lord away, and I do not know where they have put him!'

Then she turned round and saw Jesus standing there; but she did not know that it was Jesus. 'Woman, why are you crying?' Jesus asked her. 'Who is it that you are looking for?'

"Jesus said to her 'Mary!' she said to him 'My Master!'"

She thought he was the gardener, so she said to him, 'If you took him away, sir, tell me where you have put him, and I will go and get him.' Jesus said to her, 'Mary!'
(John 20:1, 11-16, GNB)

Mary came to the tomb expecting to find a cold corpse. Instead she was found by the living Jesus. Her heart was filled with sorrowful memories of him dying in weakness. Jesus delighted to give her the joyful surprise that he was no longer dead but very much alive. The husk of his humanity had not been able to contain the divine Son of God any longer. In the grave as God touched him Jesus burst through the limitations of his manhood and revealed himself for who he was: the King of kings and Lord of lords, the Victorious One, the Saviour of the world. No wonder that, on this day, a cry of pure and joyful worship echoes around the globe:

Today, Christians everywhere can echo with thanksgiving those profound words first uttered by Job:

I know that my Saviour lives,
and at the end
he will stand on this earth.
My flesh may be destroyed,
yet from this body I will see God.
Yes, I will see him for myself,
and I long for that moment.
(Job 19:25-27, CEV)

111

Thine be the glory, risen, conquering Son,
endless is the victory thou o'er death hast won;
angels in bright raiment rolled the stone away,
kept the folded grave-clothes, where thy body lay.

Thine be the glory, risen, conquering Son,
endless is the victory, thou o'er death hast won.

Lo! Jesus meets us risen from the tomb;
lovingly he greets us, scatters fear and gloom;
let the church with gladness, hymns of triumph sing,
for the Lord now liveth, death hath lost its sting.

Thine be the glory, risen, conquering Son,
endless is the victory, thou o'er death hast won.

No more we doubt thee, glorious Prince of life:
life is nought without thee; aid us in our strife,
make us more than conquerors, through thy deathless love;
bring us safe through Jordan to thy home above.

Thine be the glory, risen, conquering Son,
endless is the victory thou o'er death hast won.

*Edmond Louis Budry (1854–1932)*
translated by *Richard Birch Hoyle (1875–1939)*


Christ is risen, Alleluia!
The stone has rolled away, Alleluia!
He is not among the dead any more, Alleluia!
He has conquered Satan by his death on the Cross, Alleluia!
He has delivered me from the penalty of sin, Alleluia!
My hope and my joy are in him, Alleluia!

The Lamb who was sacrificed is worthy to be given power, riches, wisdom, strength, honour, glory and blessing . . . AMEN.

(Revelation 5:12, 14)

> O happy fault,
> O necessary sin of Adam,
> which gained for us so great a Redeemer!
>
> *The Roman Missal*